THE INCREDIBLE
MUSIC MACHINE

THE INCREDIBLE MUSIC MACHINE

CONCEIVED EDITED AND DESIGNED BY
JACQUES LOWE

WRITTEN BY **RUSSELL MILLER**
AND **ROGER BOAR**

RESEARCHED BY **DAVID MINNS**
CAPTIONS BY **TONY LOCANTRO**
HISTORICAL RESEARCH BY **LEONARD PETTS**
PHOTO LIBRARY **JANET LORD** AND **JOHN EVANS**
COVER PAINTING BY **GRAHAM OVENDEN**

A QUARTET/VISUAL ARTS BOOK

A Quartet/Visual Arts Book
First published 1982
Quartet Books Limited
27/29 Goodge Street, London W1P 1FD

British Library Cataloguing in Publication Data

Miller, Russell
  The incredible music machine.
  1. EMI
  I. Title   II. Lowe, Jacques
  338.7'6178991   HD9999.P43G7

ISBN 0-7043-2324-9

To Renee, who made me play the violin at five
but somehow didn't succeed in creating a musical
genius . . . in spite of perfect pitch

Jacques Lowe

CONTENTS

Sarah Bernhardt, the first great recording artist.

THE BIRTH OF
THE TALKING MACHINE

The President of the United States could not believe his eyes or ears. The metal box on the White House table was talking to him. It was asking about his health, informing him that it felt quite well, then bidding him a cordial goodnight. Even though it was long past midnight, President Rutherford Hayes insisted on rousing his wife and the ladies from their beds, so they could come and listen with him. It was half-past three in the morning before he would let the man who had brought the box leave.

That man was Thomas Alva Edison. And he had just invented what men had dreamed of creating for centuries, a machine capable of reproducing the human voice. Others had toyed with the challenge of preserving for posterity the fleeting moments of great music performances and the voices of famous people. But their ideas had never worked. Now Edison had produced a machine which could record sounds and play them back. And it had happened almost by accident.

Edison was thirty years old and already an inventor of distinction. Teachers at his school in Port Huron, Michigan, had dismissed him as educationally sub-normal, and after only three months' formal training his mother had taken over his upbringing, instilling in him an enthusiasm for engineering and physics, and cultivating his brilliant, restless, inquiring mind. As a boy, Edison had combined the activities of printing and selling a newspaper on a moving train with chemistry experiments in one of its carriages. When one of his concoctions exploded, the railroadmen threw him off the train at the next station. He landed heavily, and was left partially deaf.

Turning his attention to telegraphy, he joined Western Union as a wire operator, and began devising improved equipment. He invented a vote recorder for elections and ticker-tape machines for newspapers. While experimenting with a machine to transcribe telegrams by pricking codes on to paper, he stumbled across the discovery that was to

Thomas Edison surrounded by his assistants on the porch of his laboratory in West Orange, N.J.

revolutionize the world of entertainment. Under certain conditions, he noted, his telegram machine gave off a hum not unlike the human voice.

Twenty years earlier, a Frenchman, Edouard-Léon Scott de Martinville, had found a way of registering soundwaves with hog's bristle attached to a sensitive diaphragm which traced a wavy line on paper coated in lampblack. But he had been unable to reproduce the sounds.

Edison combined the principle of the Frenchman's invention with his own 'humming machine' and was encouraged by the results. On 18 July 1877 he wrote in his diary: 'Just tried experiment with diaphragm . . . the speaking vibrations are indented nicely and there

Thomas Edison with his first phonograph

is no doubt that I shall be able to store up and reproduce automatically at any future time the human voice perfectly.' In November, he produced a rough sketch of a machine he wanted his assistant John Kreusi to build and scrawled across the corner: 'Kreusi, make this.' It was startlingly simple. A brass cylinder about four inches long was attached to a threaded spindle with a handle at one end. On each side of the cylinder were two tubes fitted with needles (one to make the recording, the other to play it back) and screws to adjust their contact with the cylinder. As the handle was turned, the cylinder moved slowly between the two tubes. By December, Edison was ready to demonstrate his invention – he called it a 'phonograph' – in his laboratory at Menlo Park, New Jersey. Assistants crowded round as he leaned intently over his bench making last-minute adjustments. (Of course, he had already spoken into the phonograph and his words were now to be played back.) Satisfied at last, he began to turn the handle. As the spindle jerked the cylinder into action against one of the needles, the scratchy but unmistakable voice of Edison was heard reciting: 'Mary had a little lamb, its fleece was white as snow. . .'

'*Gott im Himmel!*' shouted Kreusi, 'it have spoke!' Even Edison would later admit: 'I was never so taken aback in my life.' The astounded assistants stayed up most of the night, singing and reciting into the machine and playing back their voices.

Early in 1878, Edison took his phonograph to the offices of that august journal, *Scientific American*, and so many people crowded in to hear the wondrous machine that there were real fears of the floor collapsing. Newspapers next day were full of the sensational invention.

12

The new-fangled talking and singing machine, called the phonograph, proved ▶ to be the sensation of the Paris Exposition of 1889.

VISITORS TO THE PARIS EXHIBITION LISTENING TO THE PHONOGRAPH.

This grasping, hurrying, money-getting, money-spending, money-boasting, mechanically inventive, successfully scientific, semi-philosophical, sham - religious, sensationally curious, and inquisitive nineteenth century feels the need of new entertainments. Those who were children fifty years ago may remember a little book called "Endless Amusement," which contained some hundred prescriptions for playing simple tricks of chemistry, optics, acoustics, magnetism, and such electricity as was then known, with small dodges in the use of cheap machinery, by which ingenious persons could astonish their juvenile acquaintance. You were told how to raise the apparition of a ghost by the aid of a mirror, a lens, and a sheet of clear glass; how to kindle a flame on a surface of water by a bit of potassium; how to make liquid in a bottle suddenly

locomotion on land and water; it outdoes the steam-engine, works for us, writes for us, turns night into day, and tells us all manner of secret terrestrial processes, as well as the news of all the civilised world. It is as ready as ever to play with us; and so is that other modern scientific invention, the telephone, the combined result of advanced acoustics and refined mechanics, by which tones and articulate syllables of speech are repeated at great distances, and in the **phonograph** are preserved for future repetition anywhere **you** please.

The "Bonne" with the Telephone.

change its colour; how to set crumbs jumping on a plate; how to make voices come from the chimney or the ceiling by "ventriloquism"; how to thrill the nerves of your neighbour with a shock from a jar of sulphuric acid containing certain metal plates. Some of us read Joyce's "Scientific Dialogues," and fancied ourselves as great conjurers as any of the ancient "Witches, Warlocks, and Magicians," whose pretended mystical gifts are specified in a recently published volume by Mr. Davenport-Adams. The wisest investigators of physical science, however, when our old men were little boys, did not know certain things which every little boy now sees or hears of in the common course. Electricity, then a mere toy in practice and a theory to account for thunder and lightning, is applied to the transmission of our messages, the illumination of our streets, houses, and ships, and the apparatus of

She claps her hands to applaud the Music.

Hearing the Music at the Opéra Comique.

Suddenly everyone wanted to see and hear it and crowds flocked to Menlo Park in such numbers that the Pennsylvania Railroad had to lay on special trains. Then came the invitation from Washington to demonstrate the machine to members of Congress and the President.

Not surprisingly, many people suspected that some kind of trickery was involved. *Scientific American* reported: 'No matter how familiar a person may be with modern machinery, or how clear in his mind the principles underlying this strange device may be, it is impossible to listen to this mechanical speech without his experiencing the idea that his senses are deceiving him.'

A bishop of the Methodist Episcopal Church was less charitable and hurried to Menlo Park, determined to prove Edison a fraud. He asked if he might record a few words himself, then rapped out a string of Biblical names at immense speed. Only when they were played back was he convinced. 'There isn't another man in the United States who could recite those names with such rapidity,' he told the inventor.

Edison took out a patent on the phonograph and in January 1878, the Edison Speaking Phonograph Company was set up to market the invention as an office dictating machine. Despite the initial excitement, the venture was not a success. The public soon lost interest in what they considered an amusing novelty. Edison admitted that the machines were too expensive and too complicated for most people's needs, and he lost interest too, switching to the challenge of devising an efficient electric light.

Not everyone forgot the phonograph. In April 1881, Alexander Graham Bell, Chichester Bell and Charles Sumner Tainter set up the Volta Laboratories to study the science of recording and reproducing sound. In 1885, they asked Edison if he would like to collaborate with them, but he declined. Two years later, they unveiled a new recording machine with a much-improved sound quality. Their 'graphophone' used wax cylinders instead of the limited-life tin foil that Edison had started with, and a sapphire stylus instead of his crude needles. A year later, Edison was back in the sound market, offering an 'improved phonograph' which also used wax cylinders, but which was powered by current drawn from large batteries instead of the graphophone's foot treadle. The Bells and Tainter immediately sued, claiming their patents had been infringed. Edison counter-sued, and so began the first of the bitter court battles that were to become the bane of the recording industry over the years to come. Neither side won, each on separate occasions being awarded one dollar damages with costs. The litigation ended only when Pittsburgh entrepreneur Jesse H. Lippincott bought the rights to both processes and set up the North American Phonograph Company.

Edison decided to market his improved phonograph in Europe. He sent a colourful ex-cavalry colonel called George Gourard to London. Lavish parties were thrown at a house in Sydenham to which Gourard invited influential people – 'to meet Mr Edison'. When they had all assembled, he played them a wax cylinder of the inventor reading a greeting to his

British friends. It was a tremendous hit. Prime Minister W. E. Gladstone sent back a message as 'a testimony to the instruction and delight I have received from your marvellous invention'. The poet Robert Browning, the Prince of Wales and other Victorian notables also recorded eulogies, and at the Paris Exposition of 1889 fashionable ladies shamelessly elbowed their way through the queue to hear the amazing 'talking' machine.

The composer Sir Arthur Sullivan heard it at Sydenham in October 1888 and said: 'I can only say that I am astonished and somewhat terrified at this evening's experiments. Astonished at the wonderful power developed – and terrified at the thought that so much hideous and bad music may be put on record for ever.' The application of his machine for music and the arts was not a consideration that endeared itself to Edison's scientific mind and he was furious when, in 1890, he found out that some of the companies who had bought a franchise to market the phonograph were selling it to fairgrounds and penny arcades. For a nickel in the slot, you could hear such varied recordings as those of the United States Marines Band playing marches by its famous conductor John Philip Sousa, selections by Mr John York Attlee 'the famous artistic whistler', 'Turkey In De Straw' by minstrel comedian Billy Golden, or a performance of 'The Whistling Coon', by George W. Johnson.

Each of the cylinder recordings was an original. Though a battery of twenty machines could be set up for a recording session, there was no way of duplicating master copies. As the number of nickel-in-the-slot phonographs grew, and people began installing talking machines in their homes, demand for cylinders increased and artists often had to repeat a performance fifty, sixty, even seventy times. Singers sang until they were hoarse. Accompanists played until they dropped.

Early phonograph catalogues listed a 'Professor Gaisberg' as one of the accompanists. He was, in reality, a bespectacled Washington schoolboy named Fred Gaisberg. Fascinated by the whole strange business of recording, he earned pocket-money playing the piano behind the early singers and when he left school in 1891 he joined a phonograph company. For a weekly wage of $10, he had to discover new artists ready to record, load the studio machines with cylinders, set up the recording horns, play accompaniments, then go round the phonograph parlours to install the newly waxed tunes. He had not been in the business long when a friend suggested he should pay a visit to a 'funny German' who was experimenting with a flat-disc talking machine. The German's name was Emile Berliner. The machine he was experimenting with was called a gramophone. Fred made the visit, and the rest is history . . . the remarkable history of the incredible music machine.

The first gramophone, where the turntable has replaced the cylinder.

'Gramophone: a talking machine wherein a sound is first traced into a fatty film covering a metal surface and which is then subjected to the action of an acid or etching fluid which eats the record into the metal. This record being a continuous wavy line of even depth is then rotated and not only vibrates the reproducing sound chamber but also propels the same by the hold its stylus retains in the record groove. The original record can be duplicated ad infinitum *by first making an electrotyped reverse or matrix and then pressing the latter into hard rubber, celluloid or similar material which is soft when warm and quite hard when cold.' – Emile Berliner, 1896.*

'Etching the Human Voice: The Berliner Invention of the Gramophone', by Raymond R. Wile.

THE MAN WHO MADE THE MUSIC MACHINE

Emile Berliner arrived in the United States on 11 May 1870, just one of millions of European immigrants seeking a fresh start in the New World. The nineteen-year-old from Hanover had no obvious skills – and very little education. For five years he drifted from town to town, and job to job, working some of the time as a commercial traveller selling haberdashery from Mississippi riverboats. In 1875, he reached New York, still rootless and penniless, and he found work as a handyman in the laboratories of the man who had discovered saccharine, Doctor Constantine Fahlberg. The laboratory fascinated Berliner, and he began to study in his spare time, reading every book he could lay his hands on. A volume called *Synopsis Of Physics And Meteorology* particularly intrigued him and he read the chapters on acoustics and electricity over and over again.

After a year in New York, he moved to Washington, working by day at a dry goods store on Seventh Street, and spending his evenings and weekends in pursuit of the new passion of his life: scientific research and experiment. He turned his bedroom, on the third floor of a boarding house, into an improvised workshop, and began to try and devise improvements for the newly invented telephone. Within a year he had developed a new kind of transmitter which offered clearer sound and increased the machine's range from two and a half to thirty miles. The Bell Telephone Company gave him $75,000 cash and the promise of $5,000 a year for all rights. He invested the money in a big brick-and-stone house on Columbia Heights, two miles north of the White House, and converted an upstairs room into a laboratory, where he turned his attention to Edison's talking machine. He was impressed by it, but was convinced that it could be made even better. He explored the ideas of other scientists, and discovered a paper written by one, Charles Cros, in 1877 and lodged with the Academy of Sciences in Paris. Cros' recording process was similar to that suggested by Edouard-Léon Scott de Martinville, but Cros suggested recording on a flat glass disc, not on a cylinder.

17

Berliner started to experiment with the idea that Cros had never had the funds to exploit. He built a hand-driven turntable and made a recording on a round glass plate blackened over a candle flame. He found that the sound quality of a groove made with a side-to-side action was far superior to the up-and-down indentations of the cylinder and the groove also held the stylus in place when the disc was re-played. After countless tests on different materials, Berliner perfected a technique of recording on to a zinc disc coated with a film of beeswax and benzine. When the disc was plunged into an acid bath, a groove was etched in the zinc. But – even more important – a reverse matrix could be made from the disc, turning the recorded track into a raised spiral edge. From this master, hundreds of duplicate discs could be pressed. This was what gave the gramophone an unbeatable advantage over the phonograph, with its non-copiable cylinders. In September 1887, Berliner applied for a patent for the invention which would lead to a multi-million-pound international industry and take music into the homes of all people, in every corner of the earth.

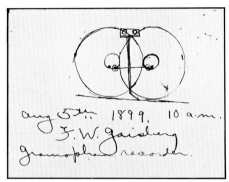

Fred Gaisberg's sketch
for gramophone improvement.

Young Fred Gaisberg received a warm welcome from Berliner when he arrived at the latter's door with his friend Billy Golden, the minstrel singer, and was delighted when Berliner suggested that they make a record on his new equipment. 'Emile placed a muzzle over Billy's mouth and connected this up by a rubber hose to a diaphragm,' Gaisberg wrote later. 'I was at the piano, the sounding board of which was also boxed up and connected to a diaphragm by a hose resembling an elephant's trunk. Berliner said, "Are you ready?" and, upon our answering "Yes", he began to crank like a barrel-organ, and said "Go".

'The song finished, Berliner stopped cranking. He took from the machine a bright zinc disc and plunged it into an acid bath for a few minutes. Then he wiped and cleaned the disc. Placing it on a reproducing machine, also operated by hand like a coffee-grinder, he played back the resulting record from the etched groove. To our astonished ears came back Billy Golden's voice. Acquainted as I was with the tinny, unnatural reproduction of the old cylinder-playing phonographs, I was spellbound by the beautiful round tone of the flat gramophone disc. Before I departed that day, I extracted a promise from Berliner that he would let me work for him when his machine was ready for development.'

Berliner kept his promise. In 1893 he launched the United States Gramophone Company in Washington, to demonstrate the potential of his invention and raise enough money to exploit it throughout the world, and he hired Gaisberg as talent-scout and accompanist.

Eldridge Johnson's patent of spring motor which regulated turntable speeds, affording even reproduction quality. ►

(2ⁿᵈ Edition)

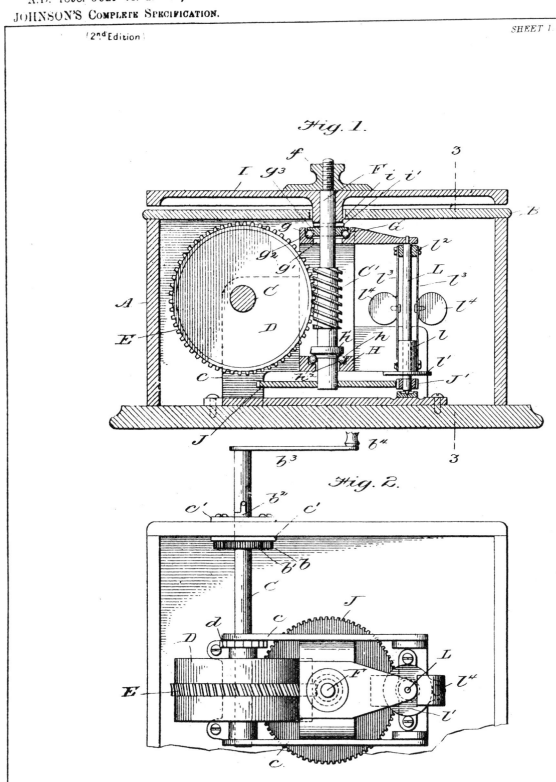

Fig. 1.

Fig. 2.

Fred was in his element. He already knew most of the important phonograph artists – singers with loud, clear voices that were ideal for recording like Irish tenor George J. Gaskin, baritone Johnny Meyers and comedian Dan Quinn. They were taken into the studio to wax such popular numbers as 'Down Went McGinty To The Bottom Of The Sea' and 'Sweet Marie'.

But professional entertainers expected fees that proved rather exorbitant for the fledgling company, so Gaisberg scoured the beer cellars of Washington for promising amateurs. On the corner of Seventh Street and Pennsylvania Avenue, he found a man clad in a threadbare coat, with a flowing tie and wide-brimmed stetson, selling a quack liver cure to a spellbound crowd. George Graham was a persuasive talker and people were rushing to hand over their nickels and dimes for bottles of coloured water. Graham turned out to be a recording natural, producing some classic recitations. One favourite was a lecture on alcohol which began: 'Drink is an evil habit. All my life I've devoted to putting drink down, and I'm *still* putting it down. . .'

The company's catalogue included work by Berliner himself. He had recorded 'The Lord's Prayer' and a guttural version of 'Tvinkle, tvinkle liddle star, how I vonder vat you are' in Germany, claiming his thick German accent would not matter, because people knew the words anyway. Gaisberg and Berliner also improvised a record called 'Auction Sale Of A Piano' one day when business was slack. 'He did the auctioneering and called out to me, "Professor, show dem vat a beautiful tone dis instrument has",' Gaisberg recalled. 'When no bids were forthcoming, he complained with anguish in his voice: "Why, ladies and gentleman, on dis piano Wagner composed *Die Götterdämmerung*. Still no bids? I see you know nothing about music. Johnny, hand me down dat perambulator." '

The company also tried to attract revenue by touting the gramophone as an advertising medium. An 1894 statement declared: 'Nobody will refuse to listen to a fine song or concert piece or oration, even if interrupted by the modest remark, "Tartar's Baking Powder Is Best", or "Wash The Baby With Orange Soap".' But raising capital remained a problem. The established phonograph, unresolved legal squabbles over patents, and a widespread belief that talking machines could never be more than toys made potential investors reluctant to risk their money. When Berliner sent Gaisberg to Boston to demonstrate the gramophone to directors of the Bell Telephone Company, they burst out laughing when they heard 'Twinkle, Twinkle Little Star'. 'Has poor Berliner come down to this?' they asked.

At last, in the autumn of 1895, a Philadelphia business syndicate agreed to put up $25,000. It was not much, but it was a start and the Berliner Gramophone Company was set up to manufacture record players and discs on a larger scale. Sales during the first year were disappointing. One of the problems was that gramophones were still hand-driven, and the quality of sound depended very much on the listener's skill at winding the turntable. A manual given to each gramophone buyer explained that seventy revolutions a minute was the ideal speed, without suggesting how this could best be achieved. It also contained precise instructions for listening to music with your *teeth*! 'To get the best results,' it said, 'procure a stick and tie a thick darning needle to one end. Stop the ears with cotton wads, place the other end of the stick between the teeth and press the needle lightly into the recording groove.'

In the summer of 1896 a brilliant young engineer came up with the breakthrough Berliner needed. Eldridge Johnson designed and constructed a spring motor for gramophones which was cheap, quiet and reliable. Soon, his little one-storey workshop in Camden, New Jersey, was in full production and, with a clockwork drive to regulate turntable speed, sales of gramophones picked up month by month. In October 1896, Berliner appointed Frank Seaman exclusive sales agent in the US for the gramophone. The latter founded The National Gramophone Company, with its headquarters in New York. By Christmas, demand was so great that sales were limited only by Johnson's ability to supply enough components. Frantic advertising and promotion campaigns by the phonograph makers failed to stem the tide and gramophone recording studios were opened in Philadelphia and New York to ensure a constant supply of new discs for the ever-increasing market.

Berliner was now ready to extend his operations. In July 1897, William Barry Owen, a young lawyer who was Sales Director of The National Gramophone Company in New York, set sail for England. His mission: to introduce the gramophone to Europe.

Emile Berliner

Orange N.J. January 17 1899

To whom it may concern —

Mr Alfred Clark of New York, the bearer of this letter, is making a visit to Europe for the purpose of introducing the apparatus and specialities, manufactured by this Company of which I am the sole proprietor. Any information afforded him will be much appreciated by me

Thomas A Edison

Thomas Edison's letter of introduction for Alfred Clark, later to become Chairman of The Gramophone Company.

THE GRAMOPHONE COMES TO EUROPE

Emile Berliner had been quite specific in the instructions he gave his young emissary to England: he was to sell all European rights to the gramophone for a considerable sum. Figures of £200,000 were mentioned. But William Barry Owen soon found that the streets of Victorian London were not paved with gold; nor were they teeming with businessmen anxious to invest in strange new inventions.

The enthusiastic American arrived in the English capital late in July 1897, and took a room at the fashionable Hotel Cecil in the Strand. He wasted no time in contacting influential people in the City and fashionable society, inviting them to lunch or dinner at his hotel after which he would demonstrate the gramophone to them, enthusing over its glorious future and its potential as a money-spinner. His guests listened politely, promised to think about it, and thanked him for his hospitality. He never heard from any of them again.

Weeks, months went by without a single offer. As London celebrated Queen Victoria's Diamond Jubilee, the disconsolate American began to wonder if he would ever make a sale. His task was not helped by the law suits that were raging back home in America at that time. Everyone was using the courts in a mad scramble to secure a profitable slice of the new recording business. Writs flew back and forth in an endless series of wrangles over patents and rights. Even before Owen had arrived in London, the Edison Bell Phonographic Company Limited was claiming that the gramophone infringed patents it had taken out, and unresolved actions such as that were an effective deterrent for potential investors in England. Berliner kept sending encouraging messages. 'I trust you will keep entirely cool, and pooh-pooh the Phonograph pretences,' he wrote in November, but it must have been hard for the young lawyer not to pack his bags in despair and head for home.

By autumn, the price for European rights to the gramophone had dropped

THE
GRAMOPHONE COMPANY Lᴰ

INCORPORATED UNDER THE COMPANIES ACTS, 1862 TO 1898.

N° OF CERTIFICATE.
2

N° OF SHARES.
1

CAPITAL £150,000,
IN 150,000 SHARES OF £1 EACH.

FIRST ISSUE OF 100,000 SHARES.

This is to Certify that *William Barry Owen*
of *15. Bayswater Terrace. Hyde Park. London* is the
Registered Proprietor of *one* Shares
fully paid, numbered *2* both inclusive
in the Gramophone Company Lᵈ subject to the Memorandum
and Articles of Association.

Given under the Common Seal of the said Company,
the *twelfth* day of *October* 18 *99*

DIRECTORS.

SECRETARY.

dramatically. Now, there was no more talk of high-powered syndicates raising hundreds of thousands of pounds. Owen was running short of money and becoming desperate. In November he opened negotiations with a number of City businessmen. When they pulled out of the talks a month later, Owen asked their legal adviser, Trevor Williams, a young Lincoln's Inn solicitor, if *he* would be interested. Williams took a gramophone home and tinkered with it for an evening and handed it back to Owen the next morning, saying he was unimpressed. But Owen detected a hint – nothing more – of interest. When he heard that Williams was leaving on a business trip to New York, the American borrowed money from a friend at the Hotel Cecil and booked a passage on the same ship. He was convinced that a week together on a transatlantic liner would give him enough time to persuade Williams to change his mind – and he was right.

In America he introduced the English solicitor to Berliner and what Berliner told Williams about the growing gramophone industry removed any lingering doubts. When Williams returned to London, he and three friends arranged a bank guarantee of £5,000. It was a far cry from the riches Owen had dreamed of, but it was enough to get the business off the ground, and he was in no position to hold out for more.

An agreement was signed on 23 February 1898 setting up a small private company called The Gramophone Company. Trevor Williams had overall control, and William Barry Owen was general manager. Gramophones would be assembled in London, from components supplied by America. The company would make its own recordings, but the actual records would be pressed at a factory in Hanover, Germany, owned by Berliner's brother. Emile Berliner had at first wanted the London organization to sell the records he was making in America, but Williams put his foot down and insisted on selecting his own repertoire – he could not envisage 'Steamboat Comin' Round De Bend' or 'The Whistling Coon' as big sellers in Victorian salons.

The new company was formed in April and in May moved into offices at 31 Maiden Lane, just off the Strand. It was a scruffy building, part of which was still being used as a third-rate hotel, but it had the advantage of being close to most of London's theatres and music-halls. As yet Williams and Owen had no way of making records – Emile Berliner was not yet ready to enlarge the elite circle of those who knew how the process was done. Instead, he sent his trusty aide Fred Gaisberg to England to start the new company's catalogue.

Fred set sail on 1 July 1898 aboard the Cunard liner *Umbria*, bound for Liverpool. 'My baggage,' he noted in his diary, 'consisted of a complete recording outfit plus a $25 bicycle with pneumatic tyres, and a notebook stuffed with addresses and advice in Berliner's own handwriting. Berliner's chief concern was to safeguard his interests from intriguing associates, and as his personal agent I was entrusted with the secrets of his recording process. This was a serious responsibility. . .'

In London, Gaisberg, then just twenty-five, was met by Owen and taken to dinner at the Trocadero Grill. As he tucked into strawberries and cream, Gaisberg jotted down the

◄ Top: William Barry Owen's share certificate.

◄ Bottom: Fred Gaisberg and family on S.S. *Umbria* on the way from New York to London.

name of the restaurant orchestra in his notebook. Before the month was out, it was making records. Gaisberg created a studio at Maiden Lane in what had been the old hotel's smoking-room. To cut the master disc, the equipment – with the huge recording horn projecting from it – was arranged on a table in the centre of the room. An upright piano stood close by on a movable platform.

By the end of July, Fred was ready to go to work. He had no trouble finding someone to try out the new studio on 2 August 1898. The Gramophone Company's offices were right next door to Rule's Restaurant, a favourite haunt of music-hall stars, and the barmaid, a girl called Syria Lamonte, fancied herself as something of a singer. In the years immediately following, more illustrious names were to join her in the new company's catalogue. Top stars such as Dan Leno, Ada Reeve, Vesta Victoria, Albert Chevalier, Vesta Tilley and Marie Lloyd took to dropping into the studio to make a record after a good lunch at Rule's. Often, they would arrive in a convivial mood, and a crate of stout was always available during recording sessions to make sure they stayed that way. Gaisberg was constantly amazed at the number of empty bottles that accumulated by the end of the day. He noted that Harry Fay generally downed six bottles, but added: 'Some of the ladies ran him a close second.'

Music-hall artists had few reservations about recording, and their powerful, robust voices, accustomed to belting out songs in gas-lit theatres for noisy audiences, made the best records. To get the best results on his primitive equipment, Gaisberg asked singers to move close to the recording horn for the low notes, and lean back for the high ones. If they forgot, he would stand behind them, shoving them forward and pulling them back at the appropriate moments.

Fat, jolly comedian Bert Shepard was one of the music-hall men who recorded almost his entire repertoire for The Gramophone Company – negro airs, English and Irish ballads, parodies, yodels and comic patter. His version of 'The Laughing Song' was still selling forty years later. But the great Dan Leno did not take to the new medium quite so readily. Without the inspiration of an audience, he dried up completely when he came face to face with the recording horn. He could not sing or speak, or crack a joke. Shamefacedly, he offered to try a dance. Fine, said Gaisberg. So Leno clambered on to a table in front of the horn and recorded his Lancashire clog-dancing routine. The next time he came to the studio, Gaisberg had taken the precaution of filling it with friends to provide an audience. The great man instantly felt more at home, and happily produced a large number of fine recordings.

By the autumn, The Gramophone Company had assembled enough gramophones and pressed enough discs to start business. In 1901, Owen started taking full-page advertisements in the national press and orders began to flood in almost immediately. Extra clerks were hired to handle the rush, though some knew little about music. A dealer who asked for some music by Mozart was less than pleased when he received 'Imitation Of

Ada Reeve, the delightful entertainer whose long career spanned
◄ music hall, musical comedies and films.

Vesta Tilley, the greatest of the music-hall male impersonators. A performer of immense vitality as well as charm, she immortalized such songs as 'Jolly Good Luck to the Girl who Loves a Sailor', 'After the Ball' and 'Following in Father's Footsteps'.

Eugene Stratton as the 'Dandy Coloured Coon'.

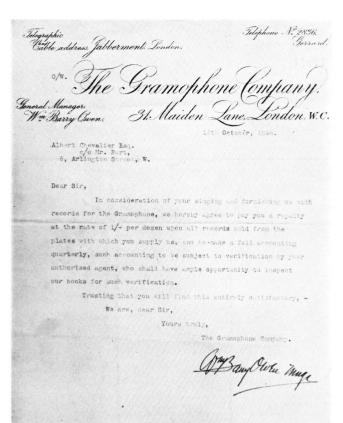

Dan Leno, renowned for his talents as a dancer, character actor and female impersonator.

Albert Chevalier, whose music-hall impersonations of the archetypal cockney became classics of the genre.

George Robey

Marie Lloyd, Queen
of British music-hall.
With her sly wink and
saucy style, she
epitomized the lively
and down-to-earth
spirit of late-
Victorian music-hall.

George Robey, the
'Prime Minister of
Mirth', one of the best
loved and most
versatile British
entertainers. His 1916
recording of 'If You
Were the Only Girl in
the World' was a best-
seller and the song
has now become an
evergreen.

Railway Trains On A Side Drum' by George Mozart, a music-hall entertainer. (Gaisberg later recalled Mozart's first appearance at Maiden Lane: 'He arrived in a four-wheel carriage and unloaded a heavy wicker theatrical trunk. This was dragged into the studio and I asked George to rehearse while I continued my preparations. After what I thought was a rather long lapse of time, I looked into the studio to find him standing before the trumpet in full make-up, complete with red nose, whiskers and costume. With difficulty I explained to him that he need not have troubled. . .')

Gaisberg's recording schedule was hectic, and it needed to be. There was an over-whelming demand for gramophones and new songs to play on them. By early December, The Gramophone Company's entire stock of turntables had been sold, and anxious dealers were 'sitting on the doorstep', waiting for a fresh shipment of components from Johnson's works in Camden. When it arrived the staff, from Owen to the office boy, rolled up their sleeves and worked into the early hours of the morning assembling new gramophones, their faces and hands covered in black oil. But by Christmas Eve they had again been cleaned out of both machines and records. They celebrated with a dinner at Rule's.

Businessmen who had spurned Owen's overtures two years earlier now looked on with envy as Trevor Williams announced 'stupendous' first-year sales figures averaging between £8,000 and £9,000 a month. Maiden Lane staff toiled from 8 a.m. to midnight coping with orders, and the Hanover pressing plant worked at full capacity, turning out 4,000 discs a day. With its London operations on a profitable footing, The Gramophone Company began to expand rapidly. It set up subsidiary companies in Italy and Germany, with the Berlin office also handling orders from Austria and Russia. In December 1900, the company was formally registered in Moscow. Record shops opened in most of the big cities, stocked from a pressing plant at Riga which was opened in the summer of 1902. Soon representatives from London were in Holland, Belgium and Scandinavia, organizing sales outlets there, and gramophones were being exported to Australia, South Africa, India and South America.

In May 1899, an energetic young American living in Paris persuaded The Gramophone Company to set up a subsidiary in France. Alfred Clark had begun his career running Emile Berliner's record store in Philadelphia. Sent to Paris by Thomas Edison to promote the phonograph, he was more than ready to handle gramophone orders too. By 1907 Clark had made so much money that he was able to retire, aged just thirty-two, to a château in the Loire Valley. But the idle life did not suit him. Twelve months later, when The Gramophone Company offered him the job of managing director in London, he was quick to accept. He was to remain at the head of company affairs for more than four decades.

To supply records for the new European outlets, Fred Gaisberg began a grand tour of continental capital cities, taking 'portable' recording equipment packed in six huge crates. By the beginning of 1900, the company catalogue boasted 5,000 selections in all the major European languages plus Russian, Turkish, Bohemian and Hebrew. The choice ranged from opera to choirs, bugle calls, bagpipes and drums, bands and balalaikas.

What it perhaps lacked in the way of real celebrities it made up for with sheer inventive genius. One of the most popular records, for example, was 'Departure Of The Troopship', a dramatic compilation calculated to cash in on patriotic fervour generated by the Boer War in South Africa. Made entirely in the Maiden Lane studio, it opened with the hubbub of crowds on the quayside, bands playing the troops up the gangplank, then bugles sounding the 'All Ashore'. Cries of 'Don't forget to write' were followed by the strains of 'Home Sweet Home' from the troops, gradually fading as the boat steamed into the distance. A last mournful, faraway hoot on its whistle was almost guaranteed to bring tears to the eyes.

The recording was meant to include a clap of thunder for extra dramatic effect, but a studio mishap intervened. The thunder was to be produced by whacking a sheet of iron with a giant hammer. The man holding the hammer struck out right on cue, but missed the iron sheet and floored the artist standing next to him, laying him out cold. Such were the hazards of being a music machine pioneer.

NEW
VICTOR RECORD
CATALOGUE

His Master's Voice
REG. U. S. PAT OFF

NIPPER TAKES A BOW

On 31 May 1899, a thin, bearded man walked into the front office of The Gramophone Company's Maiden Lane headquarters and made a curious request: he wanted to borrow a brass horn. He introduced himself as Francis Barraud, artist, and explained that he had painted a picture of his little dog Nipper listening to a phonograph. No one had shown much interest, so now he wanted to brighten it up by replacing the phonograph's rather dull black horn with a gleaming brass one.

Barraud produced a photograph of the painting to prove his bona fides and readily agreed when the clerk asked if he could show it to his general manager. William Barry Owen thought the picture was charming, and offered to buy it, on condition that Barraud painted out the phonograph and substituted a gramophone. The artist was delighted. He had already offered Nipper to a phonograph company as a possible advertisement, but had been told brusquely: 'Dogs don't listen to phonographs.' A deal was struck: £50 for the painting and another £50 for the copyright. As the artist was leaving, Owen asked what the picture was called. Barraud hesitated, then said rather shyly: 'His Master's Voice.'

Barraud set to work in his Piccadilly studio. He could not get rid of every trace of the phonograph, but, by the time he had finished, only a faint ghostly image was visible under the brushwork of the shiny new gramophone. Owen declared himself very pleased with the end result, and within months Nipper was appearing on The Gramophone Company's advertising and letterheads, on catalogue covers and needle boxes. Postcard reproductions were circulated to the trade to boost sales. Soon Nipper could be seen in shop windows in London, Moscow, Paris, Vienna, Milan and Berlin, although it was not until 1908 that he replaced the company's original logo, a recording angel, as the official trademark.

Recognition came earlier in America. Emile Berliner saw the picture hanging behind Owen's desk when he visited London early in 1900 and immediately registered the dog as

Nipper appears on both sides of the Atlantic to explode into the world's best-known and most ◄ recognized company symbol.

his own trademark when he returned to the States. Eventually, New Yorkers strolling down Broadway could look up to the rooftops and see a huge reproduction of Barraud's painting, more than fifty feet square, lit at night by hundreds of electric light bulbs.

Nipper was an instant hit. The little white mongrel with dark ears was to become the most famous trademark in the world, but he was missing when The Gramophone Company extended its operations to the Moslem countries, where dogs are considered impure. There, a cobra took his place on publicity material. In Italy, too, Nipper's welcome was less than enthusiastic; when Italians deride an artist's ability, they say he 'sings like a dog'.

Francis Barraud soom came to terms with being less well known than his pet. He made a comfortable living painting replicas of the picture for The Gramophone Company, often working on two copies simultaneously, allowing the paint on one to dry as he laboured on

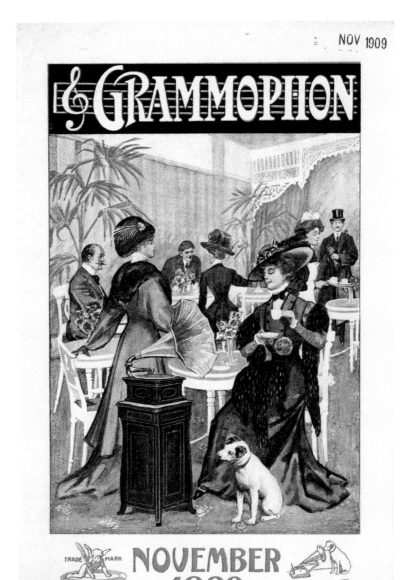

the next. In 1923 he made an exact copy of his original, first painting in a phonograph, then covering it with the gramophone. Not long afterwards, he completed a miniature version on the lid of the tiny gramophone which the Company presented for inclusion in the Queen's dolls' house.

As for Nipper, he died in 1895, four years before he became a worldwide celebrity, and long before The Gramophone Company became better known as HMV, after the title of his portrait. He was buried, it was said, under a mulberry tree in Kingston-upon-Thames. In the 1950s, company officials set out to discover the exact site of his grave. They wanted to bring his remains 'home' to the Company's new headquarters at Hayes, Middlesex. Sadly, they found that Nipper's last resting place had been covered by a concrete carpark.

گراموفون ! تیری خوش آواز پر تمام چرند پرند مشغول ہے اور میں بھی تیری آواز سنکر بینا چھوڑ دیا اور تجھے اختیار کیا

ہندوستانی ۔ فارسی ۔ پنجابی سکھ اور پشتو کے

اٹھ دس انچہ اور بارہ انچہ گراموفون کیا رڈون کی مکمل

فہرست

جسکو

دی گراموفون اینڈ ٹائپ رائٹر لمیٹڈ لندن نے

گراموفون مشینوں پر استعمال کرنے کے لیے تیار کیا ہے ۔

صدر دفتر کا پتہ

گراموفون اینڈ ٹائپ رائٹر لمیٹڈ نمبر ۷

اسپلینڈ ۔ ایسٹ ۔ کلکتہ

گراموفون

یہ ٹریڈ مارک ہر ایک گراموفون اور
ہر ایک ریکارڈ پر نمایاں ہوتا ہے

India, the dog, an unclean animal, is replaced by the cobra, with the animal kingdom as companions.

৭, ১০ ও ১২ ইঞ্চি গ্রামোফোন রেকর্ডের

তালিকা।

বাঙ্গালা, হিন্দুস্থানী ও পার্শিয়ান রেকর্ড

দি গ্রামোফোন এবং টাইপরাইটার লিমিটেড

কর্ত্তৃক

কলিকাতা।

জুলাই ১৯০৭।

দি গ্রামোফোন এণ্ড টাইপরাইটার লিমিটেড।

কলিকাতা।

"HIS MISTRESS' VOICE"

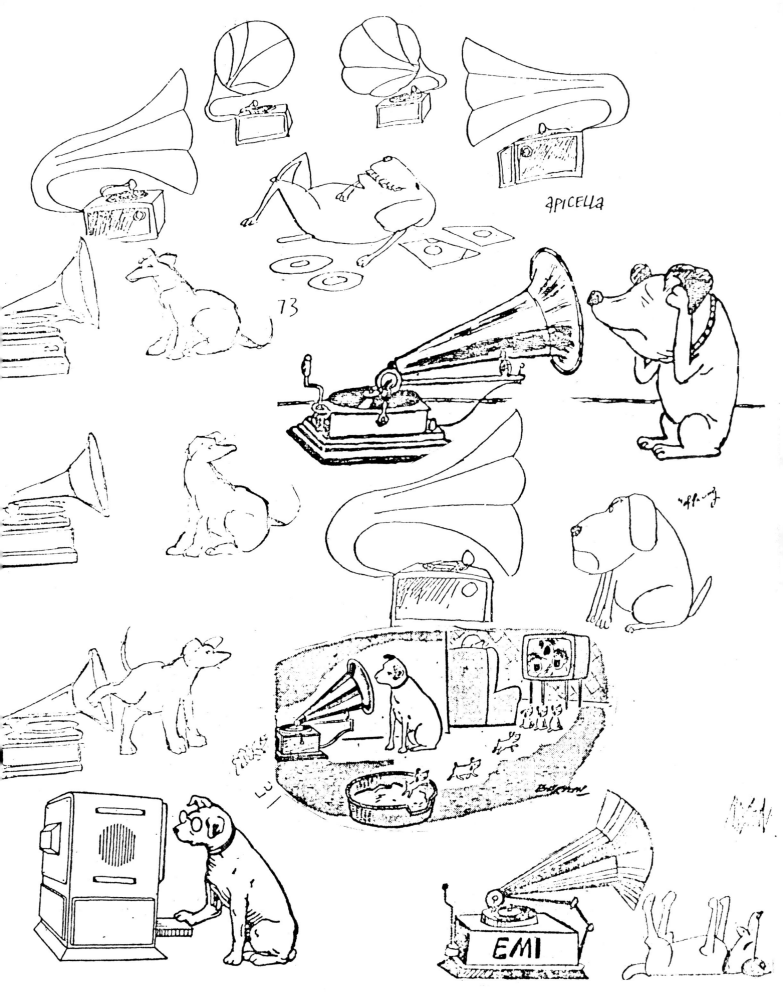

apicella

73

EMI

A CARTOON *from the* "BYSTANDER"

Drawn by FRANCIS BARRAUD, the painter of the original 'His Master's Voice'

HIS MASTER'S VOICE

Russia is taking the lion's share of Poland

HIS MASTER'S VOICE

NO! When the Terms of Peace are made
(And not long now they'll be delayed)

The Prussian hound will have no choice
He must obey His Master's Voice!

"Nipper" in a German guise! This amusing cartoon is reproduced from a recent issue of "John Bull."

A growl for His Master's Voice

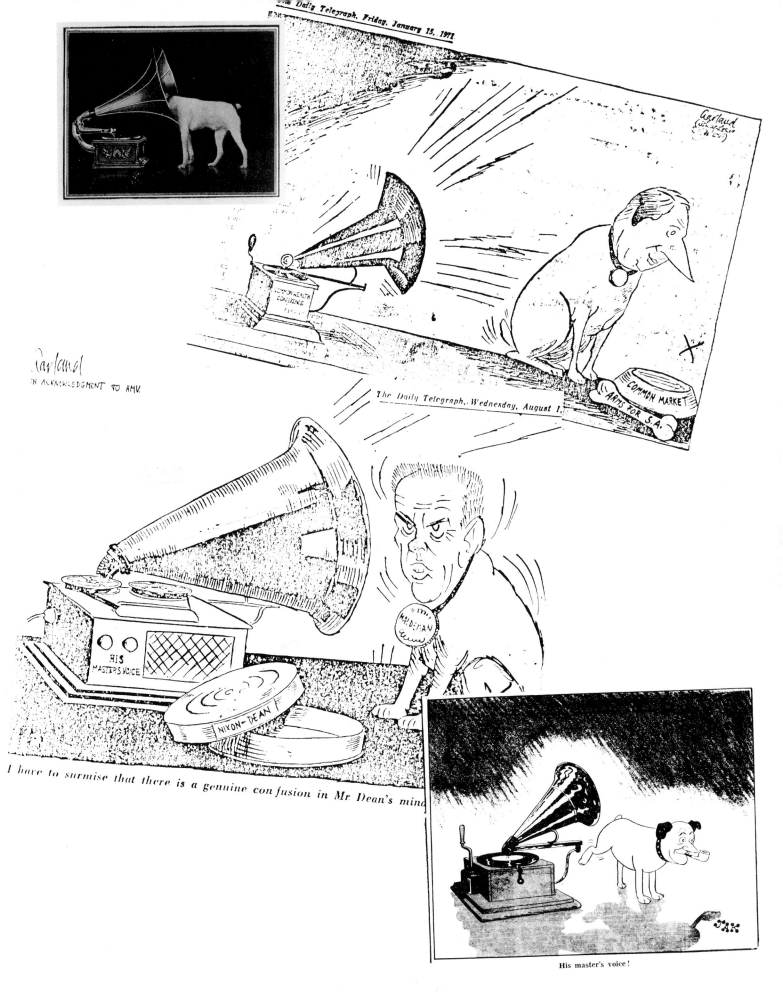

Garland
IN ACKNOWLEDGMENT TO HMV.

The Daily Telegraph, Wednesday, August 1.

COMMON MARKET
ARMS FOR S.A.

HIS MASTERS VOICE

NIXON-DEAN

I have to surmise that there is a genuine confusion in Mr. Dean's mind

His master's voice!

Columbia

GLOBE-TROTTING FOR THE RECORD

The greatest music machine pioneer of them all was Fred Gaisberg. The little man's enthusiasm for everything to do with recording was as unflagging in London as his schoolboy obsession with phonographs had been back in Washington. And when The Gramophone Company began to extend its area of influence, first in Europe and then further afield, Fred set out on marathon tours of the world's major cities, lugging along huge packing cases filled with his precious recording equipment and vast supplies of zinc blanks. He went first to Leipzig, Budapest, Vienna, Milan, Paris and Madrid; then to Stockholm, Copenhagen and The Hague in 1899. In 1900, he visited Berlin, St Petersburg and Moscow. Calcutta, Tokyo, Shanghai, Hong Kong, Singapore, Bangkok and Burma were visited in 1902–3. In one shabby hotel room after another, in one strange town after another, he would set up his apparatus and with missionary zeal persuade local singers and musicians to perform for the gramophone. If artists failed to turn up, he simply went out on to the streets and hunted up fresh talent in taverns, cafés and concert-halls. He refused to let either his own ignorance of foreign languages or the fact that many people had yet to see or hear a gramophone stand in his way.

The multi-talented Fred Gaisberg on the cello.

After each session, master recordings were sent to Hanover for pressing and The Gramophone Company quickly built up a repertoire of extraordinary range. There were military bands and gypsy ensembles, folk singers, church choirs and balalaika soloists, café

Beim verlassen Russlands um in seinen Heimath·
zurükzukehren muss jeder Fremde eine schrift-
liche Bestätigung
können, dass zum Reise ins Ausland keine Hin·
dernisse vorhanden sind

*Good only for
two years from date.*

When returning from Russia
an authorisation from the
Police is required to be produced
at the frontier or if the
was over six months—a Russ
passport

United States of America
Department of State

To all to whom these presents shall come

I, the undersigned, Secretary of State of the United States of America,

hereby request all whom it may concern to permit

F. W. Ginsberg

a Citizen of the United States

safely

and freely to pass, and in case of need to give

him all lawful Aid and Protection.

Description

Age 38 Years

Stature 5 Feet 3 Inches Eng.

Forehead   medium

Eyes   brown

Nose   medium

Mouth   mustache

Chin   pointed

Hair   black

Complexion dark

Face   oval

Given under my hand and the
Seal of the Department of State,
at the City of Washington,
the 11th day of May
in the year 1910, and of the
Independence of the United States
the one hundred and thirty-fourth.

Signature of the Bearer.

No. 27634

Fred Tyler, manager of the Tiflis office of the Russian branch.

entertainers and opera stars, recitations in dozens of different tongues and dialects, weird-sounding songs from distant lands. In some places, Gaisberg and his assistant William Sinkler Darby made as many as three hundred recordings before patiently repacking their cases and moving on.

At Maiden Lane, their progress was followed anxiously via regular wire and letter reports. From Leipzig: 'Artists here are the same as in London, and do not always keep their word. A most excellent two failed us this morning. I am interviewing two leading ladies in the opera tomorrow morning and hope to obtain their services. . .' From Moscow: 'Talent obtainable here very poor at present time of year, most people leave for country and theatres close.' From Warsaw: 'Arrived here after thirty hours' tedious travel by slow train from St Petersburg.'

Such difficulties won little sympathy from London. Instead, the intrepid travellers were harried by a stream of telegrams exhorting them to even greater efforts. A typical message from William Barry Owen was waiting when they arrived in Budapest: 'We wish for Rumanian records in all the different dialects about there that you can get. Then hurry on to Constantinople and Vienna and Milan, so that you can come along to Paris as soon as possible.'

Milan, then the mecca of the opera world, made a particularly powerful impression on Gaisberg. 'On that first recording trip I often saw the venerable Verdi, who would regularly take an afternoon drive in an open landau drawn by two horses. People would stand on the kerb and raise their hats in salute as the carriage proceeded down Via Manzoni to the park. A frail transparent wisp of a man, but the trim of his pure white beard so corresponded with the popular picture of him that one could not fail to identify him.

'One could sit at the Café Bifi in the Galleria and have pointed out Puccini, Leoncavallo, Mascagni, Franchetti and Giordano as they sauntered through the throng of chattering citizens on their way to have their mid-day aperitif.'

Gaisberg's enthusiasm for Milan was not reciprocated by the opera stars when he mentioned his gramophone. On this visit, only nonentities were keen to record. Gaisberg noted sadly: 'Whenever we approached the great artists, they just laughed at us and replied that the gramophone was only a toy.'

March 1900 found Gaisberg and the faithful Darby in St Petersburg. It was snowing hard when The Gramophone Company's local representative, an ambitious wheeler-dealer called Raphoff, met them at the railway station with a horse-drawn sleigh. After explaining that he had friends in high places, Raphoff outlined a scheme to record the voices of the Tsar and his family. The discs would be issued – at a greatly inflated price – with the Russian Imperial crest stamped on their centres, and inside a special decorative sleeve.

Gaisberg agreed to explore the possibilities. The first step was to demonstrate the gramophone at the palace of Grand Duke Michael. Gaisberg wrote: 'We drove in a sleigh, with our apparatus, to the great palace, where we were directed to the servants' entrance. We passed the guards, who examined us suspiciously, and were shown by a major-domo, with his snub Russian nose in the air, to the corner of a vast salon, furnished with chandeliers, tapestries and soft Persian carpets. With bated breath we set up our modest outfit near a Steinway grand piano.

'Just after nine o'clock, the company trooped out from the dining-room and ranged themselves round our machine. There was His Excellency, General Bobrikoff, governor of Finland, and Alexander Taneiev, the Tsarina's chancellor. Taneiev's two lovely young daughters and his two sons were also present with their mother. As they came up one by one and introduced themselves to me, I was amazed and almost ashamed at having had to come the whole way to Russia to hear such flawless English. Each of them was ready with an impromptu message for the recording trumpet. To crown all, Taneiev himself, a great musician, played one of his compositions on the Steinway. My colleague and I added a humorous touch by recording a Negro ditty.

'It was the zinc-etching process that we employed, and twenty minutes after, we played back these records to the delighted company. This was their first introduction to the miraculous talking machine.'

Unfortunately, it was an introduction that did not lead to a better acquaintance. Despite his family's interest and enthusiasm, nothing came of the project to record the Tsar.

Gaisberg was back in Russia the following summer, to try to capture Tartar music on

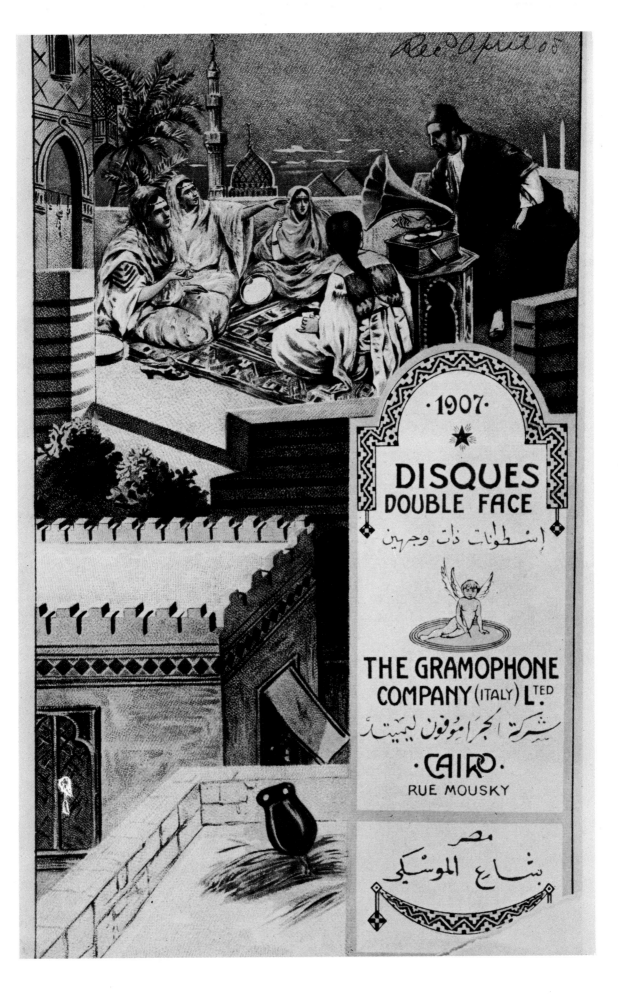

·1907·

★

DISQUES DOUBLE FACE

إسطوانات ذات وجهين

THE GRAMOPHONE COMPANY (ITALY) L.TED

شركة الجرامُوفون ليميتد

·CAIRO·

RUE MOUSKY

مصر

بشارع الموسكي

◄ Top: The travelling recording team of Fred Gaisberg and William Sinkler Darby at a recording session in Budapest. Gaisberg at the piano.

Below: Gaisberg in Japan

Their travels took them through the Middle East, Africa and the Orient. They recorded every piece of native music they could find, gave away gramophones to potentates and musicians alike and laid the foundation for The Gramophone Company's later dominant role of recording exclusivity around the world.

A Favorite Nautch Girl and her musicians.
(Armenian beweds).

Gaisberg's photo from his personal album.

disc. He took a wooden paddle-steamer up the Volga to Kazan, and booked into a hotel. The first artist to arrive was 'a petrified, yellow-skinned accordion player with a musty smell to him'. His playing was so terrible that Gaisberg offered him five roubles to stop. There followed a succession of musicians who were no easier on the nose or the ear than the first. In desperation, Gaisberg took to the streets in search of talent, and ended up in a filthy wine-shop. The singing there was so bad that the acoustic adventurer gave up the whole idea and caught the boat back to St Petersburg. This was one of the very few occasions when he admitted defeat in his recording crusade.

Safely back in London, he wrote of his Russian visits: 'I had put in six months, beginning in a zero winter of deep snow, fur coats and troikas, and finishing in a blazing summer of buzzing bees and flies. I had seen opera performance on a scale unbelievably lavish. Only the wealthiest family in the world, the Romanovs, could support them. Added to this were my first impressions of Russian music, ballet and decorative art, then at the height of their freshness and vigour. I was like a drug addict now, ever longing hungrily for newer and stranger fields of travel. Already I began to lay plans for a trip to the Far East.'

Gaisberg set out on that trip on 26 September 1902. It was the most ambitious of all his expeditions, an incredible journey which took him to India, Japan, China, Hong. Kong, Singapore, Thailand and Burma. During nearly a year away from England, he and his

◄ 1913 Chinese catalogue

assistant made a total of 1,700 recordings of the ethnic music of the bazaars and palaces, tea-houses and jungle villages. All the recordings were taken in the various town centres, the native singers being brought into town to record. And they did it in the face of enormous problems. Suspicious, difficult Customs officials caused hold-ups at every port, insisting on examining each of the thirty crates of equipment. Gaisberg found the local music universally terrible, the heat almost unbearable. Tropical diseases and strange food put them on their backs more than once. But they would not be deterred from their mission.

Arriving in Calcutta on 27 October 1902 aboard the old East Indiaman *Coromandel*, Gaisberg soon decided it was a waste of time using local British residents for making contacts. 'They might be living on another planet for all the interest they took in Indian music,' he noted. 'They dwelt in an Anglo-Saxon compound of their own creation, isolated from India.' A local police inspector proved more valuable when Gaisberg was setting out to round up talent himself, elbowing his way through unsavoury alleys, jostled by fakirs and beggars, to find native theatres and music-halls.

Gaisberg also got to know Indian businessmen, and it was at a dinner party at a rich merchant's home that he made his first signing – Goura Jan, a popular singer-dancer who had been hired to entertain his guests. She was a rather fat lady, and Gaisberg was less than charmed by her habit of chewing betel nuts and spitting out the juice, but she turned out to be one of the few outstanding artists to be discovered by him during his Indian stay. She arrived for the recording session with an entourage of five servants: one boy's sole task was to fan the great lady; another carried the silver cuspidor into which she ejected the betel juice. Gaisberg noted sourly: 'Madame Calvé [the celebrated French operatic heroine] came to our laboratory with far less cortège and required much less attendance.'

Gaisberg was glad when the time came to leave India. Apart from the dubious qualities of some of the singers, they were invariably accompanied on a missionary's organ, an instrument which produced a dull, uninspiring sound that he came to loathe.

He spent Christmas 1902 on board a P & O ship, the *Chusan*, en route to Yokohama. In Japan came one of the triumphs of the trip: a recording of the Imperial Band at the Mikado's palace. The session was set up by a British diplomat, who told the Emperor that the King of England owned a gramophone, and would undoubtedly ask to hear the Imperial Band, once he learned that The Gramophone Company had been making records in Japan. Gaisberg found the music 'weird and fascinating indeed'. He noted in his diary: 'Though they played some ten pieces, it was impossible to distinguish one tune from another.' He was also intrigued by some male singers who seemed to be great favourites of the Emperor. 'They do a kind of impassioned declaiming, using the full power of the voice and going from the lowest pitch to the highest. To me it sounded like a donkey braying.' During his stay in Yokohama, Gaisberg made 274 discs of music he mostly considered 'simply too horrible'.

Things were even worse when he reached Shanghai in March 1903 and set about collecting Chinese dialect material. 'About fifteen people had come, including the accompanying band,' he recalled. 'As a Chinaman yells at the top of his power when he sings, he can only sing two songs an evening, and then his throat becomes sore. Their idea of music is a tremendous clash and bang. On the first day, after making ten records, we had to stop. The din had so paralysed my wits that I could not think.'

Gaisberg moved on to Hong Kong, and there he ran into trouble of a different kind. 'This time the artists were principally tea-house girls,' he wrote. 'Their bound feet made it impossible for them to walk, so they were carried to our improvised studio on the shoulders of giant coolies. These girls were lacquered and painted and dressed in embroidered silks. They looked like expensive doll babies. I have reason to remember their long, coloured fingernails. Their voices have the sound of a small wailing cat, and while I was attempting to push one singer closer to the horn, she turned on me like a viper. At the same time the big coolies also attacked me. Evidently I, as a foreigner, in touching the lady, had committed a *faux pas*. After that I was more discreet in handling the tea-house girls.'

Gaisberg sent two hundred master discs off to Hanover from Hong Kong, then packed his thirty cases and himself travelled on to Bangkok, Rangoon and Singapore, adding Siamese, Javanese, Malay and Burmese repertoire to his weird and wonderful collection of sound. Then he too headed for home. Aboard the Australian steamer *Oceana* in the Mediterranean, he reviewed his trip in his diary: 'Everywhere the invention aroused the greatest interest. The native and European Press interviewed us and printed many columns about this amazing expedition. In my spare time I gave dozens of gramophone recitals to audiences who heard recorded sound for the first time.'

Gaisberg's greatest adventure had established The Gramophone Company firmly in the Far East. It had added 1,700 recordings of ethnic music to the catalogue and it had all been achieved for the paltry cost of £2,529. Fred Gaisberg arrived at London's Victoria Station on 5 August 1903 with some great stories to tell the friends who met him. But they had news for him, too. For, in his absence, exciting things had been happening in Europe.

RECORDING
THE GREAT OPERA STARS

When Sir Herbert Beerbohm Tree, the renowned actor-manager of the English theatre, was first confronted with the gramophone's recording horn, he asked disdainfully: 'Am I expected to put my beautiful voice into *that?*' It was an attitude shared by most of the great artists at the turn of the century. Despite the achievements of the infant industry, many serious singers and musicians considered the gramophone merely an amusing novelty, completely unworthy of their talents or attention. It was particularly frustrating for the record-makers, for they were living in the Golden Age of Opera, a dazzling decade boasting such giants as Caruso, Chaliapin, Melba, Patti, Tamagno.

William Barry Owen, hurt by the refusal of the great stars to take the gramophone seriously, reasoned that perhaps they could be won over by a distinguished fellow musician and he invited Landon Ronald to visit The Gramophone Company's London office to listen to the latest recordings. Ronald, at the age of twenty-seven associate conductor at Covent Garden Opera House and favoured accompanist to many of the Garden's leading soloists, was not interested. 'I wasn't a bit enthusiastic and wrote a cold letter,' he recalled. 'At that time the gramophone was a toy machine which gave forth unpleasant, grating noises. Most adults hated it.'

Owen persisted and invited the young conductor to lunch at the Savoy Hotel, after which he was persuaded to hear what the gramophone had to offer. At Maiden Lane, Owen played him 'The Devout Lover' sung by a baritone who was a friend of Ronald. It had been recorded by a new wax engraving process, which gave more faithful sound and less surface noise than the old zinc etching system, and the young conductor was astonished by the improved quality. He also recognized his friend's voice instantly. Owen the super-salesman seized his opportunity. The public would also recognize the great singers of the day, if only they would record, he said. Then, his eyes glinting with enthusiasm, he added: 'It is up to you to get them to sing and make them realize that this is *the* invention of the future.'

◄ While the elaborate gramophone cabinets sold for £12 each, the records, one-sided and each   57
playing for ten minutes went up to £1, a fortune for that time, and higher.

Antonina Neshdanova in Rimsky-Korsakov's *Sadko*

Joachim Tartakoff as Eugene Onegin.

Mattia Battistini in *Les Huguenots*

Hɛar
PADEREWSKI
The Greatest Living Pianist
PLAY IN YOUR OWN HOME

"His Master's Voice"
RECORDS

CHAS·E
DAWSON

Ronald was far from convinced he could do the job, but agreed to try. He dropped in at St James's Hall, where his friend Ben Davies, the Welsh tenor, was rehearsing for a concert. During a break, the two men exchanged small talk for a while, then Ronald casually suggested that Davies should sacrifice his normal round of golf the next morning to sing a few songs. He could earn the same fee as he would receive for an entire concert.

'Rather!' enthused Davies. 'Is some old dowager giving a morning concert?' His smile dissolved into indignation when The Gramophone Company was mentioned and he refused to consider the idea. But after Ronald pleaded with him, staking his own reputation on the quality of the new wax recording process, Davies finally agreed to trust his voice to the gramophone – for his friend's sake.

The young conductor rushed back to Maiden Lane to break the news to Owen. The American was delighted – until he learned how much money Davies had been promised for the session. 'This company is not out to house and keep concert artists,' he said frostily. 'Please remember in future that we have never paid more than ten guineas, and that generally the artist is content to make records for the mere pleasure of hearing his voice reproduced.' Owen did honour the agreement, however, and it proved cheap at the price. The Ben Davies records soon became best-sellers.

If Owen was angry at the deal Landon Ronald had arranged, he hit the roof in the autumn of 1901 when a cable arrived from the Russian branch of The Gramophone Company. The manager N.M. Rodkinson asked for between £1,000 and £1,500 to be spent on a special recording session involving four of the most celebrated stars of the Imperial Opera: Feodor Chaliapin, Anastasia Vialtseva, and the husband-and-wife team of Nicola and Medea Mei-Figner. To cover the costs, he proposed charging double the normal price when the records were released. Owen at first refused to authorize what he considered wanton extravagance, but after a series of letters between the two men, Rodkinson finally won the day with reasoned and eloquent argument. 'In Russia,' he wrote, 'as in no other country in the world, the demand exists for celebrated names on gramophone records for the simple reason that gramophones are bought mostly by the cultivated and high class of society. The addition, therefore, of celebrities to our catalogue would mean an increase not only among present owners of gramophones, but would open up new paths in the highest circles. The public will gladly pay, and the dealers are also willing, as they realize the absurdity of selling the records of an artist like Mrs Figner at the same price as records of a variety-hall singer.'

For a combined fee of slightly under £1,000, the four great artists made a total of sixty records. They were issued with red labels, to distinguish them from the discs of lesser singers and, although they cost ten shillings each, the public was more than willing to pay extra, as Rodkinson had predicted. Soon other Gramophone Company branches were looking for

◄This 1911 poster celebrates Ignace Paderewski, who accompanied many of the great opera stars. An artist and a patriot, he was one of the greatest pianists of his time and was later to become Prime Minister of his native Poland.

opportunities to make their own red-label records. Early in 1902, Alfred Michaelis, the manager in Milan, asked for some of the Russian records to be sent to him urgently. He explained: 'These would serve me for persuading celebrated singers here also to sing for the gramophone.' The celebrated singer he had particularly in mind was the sensation of La Scala, a young tenor called Enrico Caruso.

In March, Fred Gaisberg and a new assistant, his brother Will, set out for Italy to try to record Caruso. At first their efforts were thwarted – not by Caruso this time but by the Board back in London. When Fred asked permission to pay Caruso £100 for recording ten titles, the home office was horrified and forbade him to spend the money as the singer was much too expensive. Fred decided to ignore the order and within a month he had succeeded in his aim. The ten songs he put on wax during the afternoon of 11 April 1902 were later acclaimed the first completely satisfactory records ever made. More important, as Fred Gaisberg noted, was the fact that Caruso's name became the 'decoy that brought other hesitating celebrities to our recording studio'.

News of The Gramophone Company's coup spread fast, and Landon Ronald was quick to take advantage of the interest it caused. Even before the records were released in London, he had signed up most of the major artists due to perform with Caruso at Covent Garden's next International Season. They were glittering names: French bass Pol Plancon, baritones Anton van Rooy, David Bispham and Antonia Scotti, American soprano Suzanne Adams, and French operatic heroine Emma Calvé.

By the end of 1902, the Company's Red Label catalogue, printed on expensive heavy paper and lavishly illustrated with pictures of the artists, boasted 'the most enchanting selections of the world's greatest singers'. Almost all of them were stars of the opera.

During 1903, more famous names were added. Francesco Tamagno, the singer who created the role of Verdi's Otello, agreed to come out of retirement to record for The Gramophone & Typewriter Limited, as The Gramophone Company was then called. The fee was a staggering £200 per record, plus a royalty of four shillings. Some of his discs were the new twelve-inch records which increased playing time from three to four minutes a side. They sold for £1 each – a fact that Owen's advertisements presented as a positive virtue – and the facts surrounding the recording sessions were somewhat embroidered to entice the customers. 'The entire staff of our laboratories proceeded to Tamagno's Palace at San Remo, and for three weeks were guests of the great singer,' the promotional copy read. 'There we erected our latest recording plant, especially built for the occasion. In his own palace, in his own good time, and at any moment he felt it would be a pleasure to sing, and when he was in the mood to do himself justice, he made the records we now publish. To obtain it you must pay £1 – you could not expect to pay less for it.' In fact, the recording session lasted just four days. And the only reason it was held at Tamagno's house was because he flatly refused to sing in a hotel, until then the most usual site for the travelling recording studio.

Marie Michailova, the Russian soprano who made many gramophone records, although her career was uneventful and, apart from one tour of Japan, confined entirely to Russia.

Red Label recordings continued throughout the year all over Europe, and further great names were added to the catalogue: in Warsaw, Mattia Battistini, the baritone whose *bel canto* earned him the title 'La Gloria d'Italia'; in Paris, Felia Litvinnem, the statuesque diva famous for the role of Isolde. In Rome, in 1904, the second series of recordings by the choir of the Sistine Chapel and the last great castrato, Alessandro Moreschi, took place, the first series having been taken in 1902. Also in 1904, Nellie Melba finally gave in to pressure from Landon Ronald. She was to make a historic recording of the Bach–Gounod 'Ave Maria' with Czech violinist Jan Kubelik, the Red Label catalogue's first solo instrumentalist. And in 1905, the legendary Adelina Patti, the last major artist to hold out against recording, succumbed.

With the Red Label catalogue now packed with all the most glittering names of the Golden Age of Opera, the gramophone could never again be dismissed as just an amusing toy. Only seven years after the formation of The Gramophone Company, the voices of the world's greatest singers could be heard from the trumpets of music machines all over the world.

CARUSO

The première of Baron Franchetti's opera *Germania* in 1902 caused a sensation in Milan. The two young singers in the leading roles, soprano Amelia Pinto and tenor Enrico Caruso, were the toast of the town. Every seat in La Scala Opera House was booked for weeks. It was impossible to buy tickets anywhere. So when Fred and Will Gaisberg arrived in the city with their new wax recording equipment, they were delighted to discover that Alfred Michaelis, The Gramophone Company's man in Milan, had pulled strings to get them seats to hear the two stars.

All the La Scala boxes were owned by noblemen or wealthy businessmen, but Michaelis had been able to place judicious bribes in the right quarters, and had come up with a box for that evening only. It was quite a Company party for, besides the Gaisbergs, William Barry Owen, the London general manager, and Alfred Clark, then in charge of the Paris office, were in town with their wives. They all settled in their seats in the packed opera house, waiting with excited anticipation for the overture. Suddenly there came a loud tapping on the door of their box. Angrily Michaelis got up and wrenched open the door. There stood the owner of the box, equally furious, with his own guests. Heated words followed, as the Italian baron who owned the seats insisted, not unnaturally, on his right to occupy them. Michaelis, beside himself with rage, challenged him to a duel and cards were ritually exchanged. To his horror, Will Gaisberg was nominated as second, and spent a sleepless night nervously pacing the floor of his hotel room, worrying about what he would have to do. Fortunately, by morning, tempers had cooled and the duel was never fought.

A few nights later, more bribes secured seats in the stalls and the Gaisbergs finally heard Caruso sing. 'I cannot describe my transports or the wild enthusiasm of the audience,' Fred noted. 'Is it to be wondered that I lost my head? I turned to Michaelis and said, "Find out what fee he will accept for ten songs." '

Next day Caruso's manager named his terms: he wanted £100 and insisted that the session be fitted into a single afternoon. Gaisberg was shocked, but agreed the figure and fixed a date. The brothers set up their recording equipment in a large private drawing-room on the third floor of the Hotel Milan. They took the precaution of screening it with a curtain, because the wax recording process was still a trade secret and they did not want spies from rival companies to see it.

On the morning of 11 April, the Gaisbergs recorded Amelia Pinto singing arias from *Germania*. Then they waited nervously for Caruso to show up. He arrived late, accompanied by his usual retinue of hangers-on, and announced that he wanted to get the recording over quickly, so that he could get away for a meal. Fred Gaisberg was not in the least put out for he knew he had the chance to make recording history. Caruso was the 'answer to a recording man's dreams'. His rich and powerful voice was perfect for the acoustic recording system, blotting out the surface noise of the early recording process.

'The items were all about two-and-a-half to three minutes long and one after the other, as fast as we could put the waxes on the machine, Caruso poured the fresh gold of his beautiful voice on them,' Fred recalled. It took just two hours to record ten songs and Caruso was paid on the spot – the first instalment of the £1 million he would earn from making records over the next twenty years. Gaisberg confessed himself 'stunned' at the ease with which the singer earned the 'vast sum' of £100. But The Gramophone Company did not do too badly out of the session, either. Profits from the ten records were later estimated at more than £15,000.

The best of them was reckoned to be 'E Lucevan le Stelle', from *Tosca*. It led directly to Caruso being offered a contract with the New York Metropolitan Opera. Heinrich Conried, new manager of the Metropolitan, had heard Caruso sing during a visit to Europe and was anxious to engage him. But the directors in New York were not so sure of his pulling power. So Conried took a copy of 'E Lucevan le Stelle' back to America to convince them. Solely on the strength of that record, Caruso was sent a contract inviting him to appear in New York.

| Artiste | *Caruso* | Issued by | *Victor* | Branch. |

Contract dated   Runs from   to   years.

Advance on a/c of Royalty   Royalty per Record $4.20   10" $7.80   12"

Color of Label *Red*   Retail Price $2.   10" $3   12"

SALES.

BRANCH	1906 30th June Combined	1906 December 31st 10"	1906 December 31st 12"	1907 30th June 10"	1907 30th June 12"	1907 31st December 10"	1907 31st December 12"	1908 30th June 10"	1908 30th June 12"	1908 31st December 10"	1908 31st December 12"	1909 30th June 10"	1909 30th June 12"
Alexandria *Cairo*			121		94	8	53	9	45	8	64	50	96
Barcelona	9		528		457	192	706	237	669	567	907	381	719
Berlin	759		843		552	939	3711	1102	2493	2441	4705	1578	2837
Brussels	59		76	12	119	45	222	55	223	85	216	46	154
Calcutta			28	1	21	1	68		81	4	67	1	82
Copenhagen	26		115		52	44	272	25	75	104	91	73	74
London	931		1356		1687	293	3051	722	3192	631	2571	553	1810
Milan	265		368		560	214	1069	200	731	679	669	300	574
Moscow			106	20	61	31	105	60	115	246	322	297	598
Paris	132		530		444	87	436	200	843	377	964	469	995
Shipping						29	721	6	58				
Stockholm	1		67		49	10	65	16	79	50	73	37	45
Vienna	97		507	291	65								
Victor T/M Co. *Budapesth*						339	401	258		144	144	128	
St Petersburg	44		116	82	279	143	718	156	455	195	670		
Amsterdam	26		67		240								
Sydney			276	32	394								
TOTAL	2349		5104	438	5068	2375	11548	3046	9059	5531	11463	3853	7951

Royalty due on Sales

PAYMENTS.				ROYALTY EARNED.					BALANCE.		
Date	Details	£	s. d.	Date	Details	£	s.	d.	£	s.	d.
				June 1906							
				Dec ..		684	-	10			
				June 1907		710	16	6			
				Decr -		1719	1	3			
				June 1908		1433	18	1			
				Decr .		1935	8	9			
				June 1909		1343	12	11			
				December .		2095	4	0			

Caruso's first royalty sheet. He was to earn more than a million pounds from recording during his lifetime.

Enrico Caruso as Radames in *Aida*.

Ruggiero Leoncavallo, here seen with friends in 1903, provided Caruso with his most popular role, Canio in *Pagliacci*.

Giacomo Puccini was the last and probably the most
successful of all the composers of Italian opera. His
most popular works still fill the world's opera houses and
without *La Bohème*, *Madame Butterfly* and *Tosca* the
catalogues of the recording companies
would be much the poorer.

Caruso as Dick Johnson in Puccini's
The Girl of the Golden West.

Antonio Scotti, Paolo T
and Caruso

Caruso and w
always dapp
always *à la m*

CALVÉ

Among the stars appearing in the Covent Garden International Season in 1902 was Madame Emma Calvé, the celebrated French operatic heroine noted for enriching her roles with flashes of Latin temperament. From the time Landon Ronald first approached her about recording for The Gramophone Company, she led him a merry dance. First, she could not make up her mind whether she *ought* to record, then she could not decide whether she *would*. A fee of 100 guineas for six songs finally persuaded her, but Ronald's troubles were far from over.

'She was staying at the Hyde Park Hotel and I was to fetch her in a four-wheeler, take her to Maiden Lane, and accompany her on the pianoforte,' he recalled. 'After much running about for music she had forgotten, and picking up gloves she had dropped, I got her safely into the cab. I must admit that the offices in Maiden Lane at that time scarcely inspired confidence or gave the impression that they belonged to a large and prosperous company. Certainly they didn't impress her.'

As the carriage drew up outside The Gramophone Company's headquarters, the singer took one look at the dingy façade and shrieked: '*Mon Dieu*, but never in my life will I enter such a place. It is a tavern, not a manufactory! I shall be robbed there, I know it, I feel it in my bones. You have brought me to a thieves' den.'

Ronald, putting on what he later described as a 'sickly smile', was unable to persuade the increasingly hysterical artist to leave the carriage. Then he had an inspiration. He rushed into the building, collected Madame Calvé's cheque, gave it to the best-turned-out young man he could find, and told him to take it outside and present it to the great lady with all the charm and ceremony he could muster. While Ronald hovered in the doorway, the young man nervously approached the carriage. There was a moment of suspense. Then Ronald heard the famous voice trilling: '*Mais vous êtes gentil, Monsieur. Merci beaucoup. Oui, oui, oui; je vous suiverai avec plaisir.*' With that, the lady alighted from the carriage and swept into the building. As she passed Landon Ronald, she commanded: '*Venez, mon petit Ronald!*'

Once inside the basement studio, Madame Calvé made no concessions to the limitations of the recording process. She ruined several wax blanks by commenting on her performance in the middle of a song. Halfway through the *Habanera* from *Carmen*, for example, she stopped and asked Ronald if he did not agree that she was in fine voice. In the *Séguedille* from *Carmen*, she insisted on dancing in front of the recording horn, just as she did on stage, and no one could persuade her that this would spoil the recording. When she failed to reach the final high note in another aria, Fred Gaisberg slipped a second wax blank on to the turntable and she tried again. The same thing happened. '*Mon Dieu!*' she growled through clenched teeth.

Everyone in the studio was greatly relieved when the six records were at last completed. Sydney Dixon, the young man who had offered her the cheque, described 'the end of a trying day' in the company's house-magazine, *Voice*: 'Once more there was an atmosphere of *Carmen* as the hat and veil were put on, and, with half a laugh and half a sob, the great artist disappeared through the doorway. We, too, were somewhat taxed with the strain of such a recording session. Poor Mr Landon Ronald, an artist to his fingertips, sat with blanched face recovering from the whirlwind excitement of the recording. We prepared to close up for the day. On the floor by the doorway was a crumpled ball of paper. It was Madam Calvé's cheque! The biggest by far we had ever drawn in favour of an artist.'

Emma Calvé, beautiful, temperamental and imperious

Dame Nellie Melba, the Australian Diva. Melba's first recordings were made by HMV in her drawing-room at Great Cumberland Place in London in 1904, and her last included some highly effective excerpts recorded live at her Covent Garden 'Farewell' in 1926. During a long and brilliant reign over the world's leading opera houses, Melba recorded some of the most popular records of her time, including 'Ave Maria', accompanied by Jan Kubelik.

MELBA

Nellie Melba was a real prima donna – difficult, temperamental and brilliant. When, early in 1904, she finally agreed to make a record, the conditions she imposed made both Landon Ronald and Fred Gaisberg turn pale. First, she had no desire to visit The Gramophone Company's studios – the recording session would have to be held at her London home. Second, the accompaniment was to be a full-scale orchestra, nothing less. Third, she alone would decide what was to happen to the recordings. If she did not like them, they were never to be made public.

Company executives swallowed hard and agreed. On the day of the session, Ronald somehow managed to fit a 45-piece orchestra into the elegant drawing-room of Melba's house in Great Cumberland Place, and still leave enough space for Gaisberg, his assistants and their equipment. Melba showed her contempt for the whole operation with caustic comments about everything and everyone. At the end of the day, she decided she had no special wish for any of the records to be released. It had all been a complete waste of time.

Poor Landon Ronald, who had conducted the orchestra, pleaded with her to change her mind. Melba at first refused to budge. Then she told him to send one record to her old father in Australia. If he recognized her voice, she might think again. But the directors of The Gramophone Company did not intend to let Melba slip through their fingers. Sydney Dixon, the young man who had charmed Madame Calvé out of her carriage, was sent to Monte Carlo, where Melba was performing. Every night for an entire month he bombarded her with flowers, letters and dinner invitations. She ignored him.

Then Dixon heard that Melba was due to have dinner with the composer Camille Saint-Saëns. With the help of Alfred Clark, the Company's manager in Paris, he arranged secretly to offer Saint-Saëns a recording contract in return for his support. On the night of the dinner, Dixon hid in an adjoining room with a gramophone and the latest Caruso records. At what he judged to be a suitable moment, he began playing one of them. Right on cue, the old composer started to enthuse about the wonders of the gramophone. By March, Melba had weakened sufficiently to allow one of her records to be played at a Press reception, to test the reaction of music critics. It was favourable enough for her to agree to another recording session at Great Cumberland Place.

Melba finally signed an agreement with The Gramophone Company on 11 May 1904. Her demands were unprecedented: her records were to sell for a guinea – more than those of any other artist; her royalty was to be five shillings a record; and she wanted a fee of £1,000 to be paid immediately. Finally, her records were to have a distinctive mauve label, a colour that would never be given to any other singer. Wearily, the Company agreed. The one consolation was that she was prepared to record in the City Road studios; but, as it turned out, this was to be as trying as squeezing an orchestra into her drawing-room.

'There was the big Daimler sent to fetch her and her attendants,' Fred Gaisberg recalled. 'There was the youngest typist prettily dressed to hand the Diva a five-guinea bouquet of roses. The directors, in striped trousers, white spats, white waistcoats, cutaway black coats and squeaky patent-leather boots, danced attendance on her ladyship as she cracked the whip with baleful glee. My recording studio was on the top floor, but the lift would stop at the second floor where a long table was set up in the Board Room laden with good things to eat. Here, light refreshments – including the ubiquitous champagne – were partaken, and then the artists were sent on up to the studio where I would be anxiously waiting to get on with the job of making records – no easy task under these conditions.'

The first pressings of Melba's records were in the shops at the beginning of July 1904. They sold out within days. She went on to make many more records . . . but the recording sessions never got any easier.

Jan Kubelik, the legendary violinist, who accompanied Melba on some of her best-selling records.

Melba as Ophelia

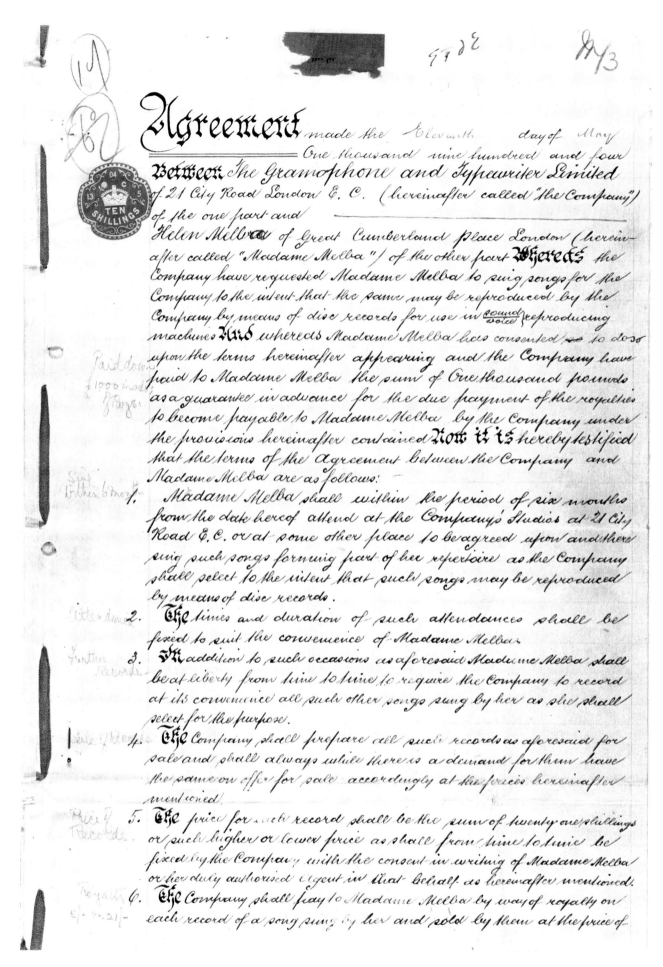

Agreement

made the Eleventh *day of* May *One thousand nine hundred and four* **Between** *The Gramophone and Typewriter Limited of 21 City Road London E. C. (hereinafter called "the Company") of the one part and* Helen Melba *of Great Cumberland Place London (hereinafter called "Madame Melba") of the other part* **Whereas** *the Company have requested Madame Melba to sing songs for the Company to the intent that the same may be reproduced by the Company by means of disc records for use in* sound voice *reproducing machines* **And** *whereas Madame Melba has consented to do so upon the terms hereinafter appearing and the Company have paid to Madame Melba the sum of One thousand pounds as a guarantee in advance for the due payment of the royalties to become payable to Madame Melba by the Company under the provisions hereinafter contained* **Now it is** *hereby testified that the terms of the Agreement between the Company and Madame Melba are as follows:*

1. Madame Melba shall within the period of six months from the date hereof attend at the Company's Studios at 21 City Road E.C. or at some other place to be agreed upon and there sing such songs forming part of her repertoire as the Company shall select to the intent that such songs may be reproduced by means of disc records.

2. The times and duration of such attendances shall be fixed to suit the convenience of Madame Melba.

3. In addition to such occasions as aforesaid Madame Melba shall be at liberty from time to time to require the Company to record at its convenience all such other songs sung by her as she shall select for the purpose.

4. The Company shall prepare all such records as aforesaid for sale and shall always while there is a demand for them have the same on offer for sale accordingly at the prices hereinafter mentioned.

5. The price for each record shall be the sum of twenty one shillings or such higher or lower price as shall from time to time be fixed by the Company with the consent in writing of Madame Melba or her duly authorised agent in that behalf as hereinafter mentioned.

6. The Company shall pay to Madame Melba by way of royalty on each record of a song sung by her and sold by them at the price of

Melba's 1904 contract calling for a guaranteed £1,000 advance, a stupendous amount of money in those days.

[VIC]TORIA 371.

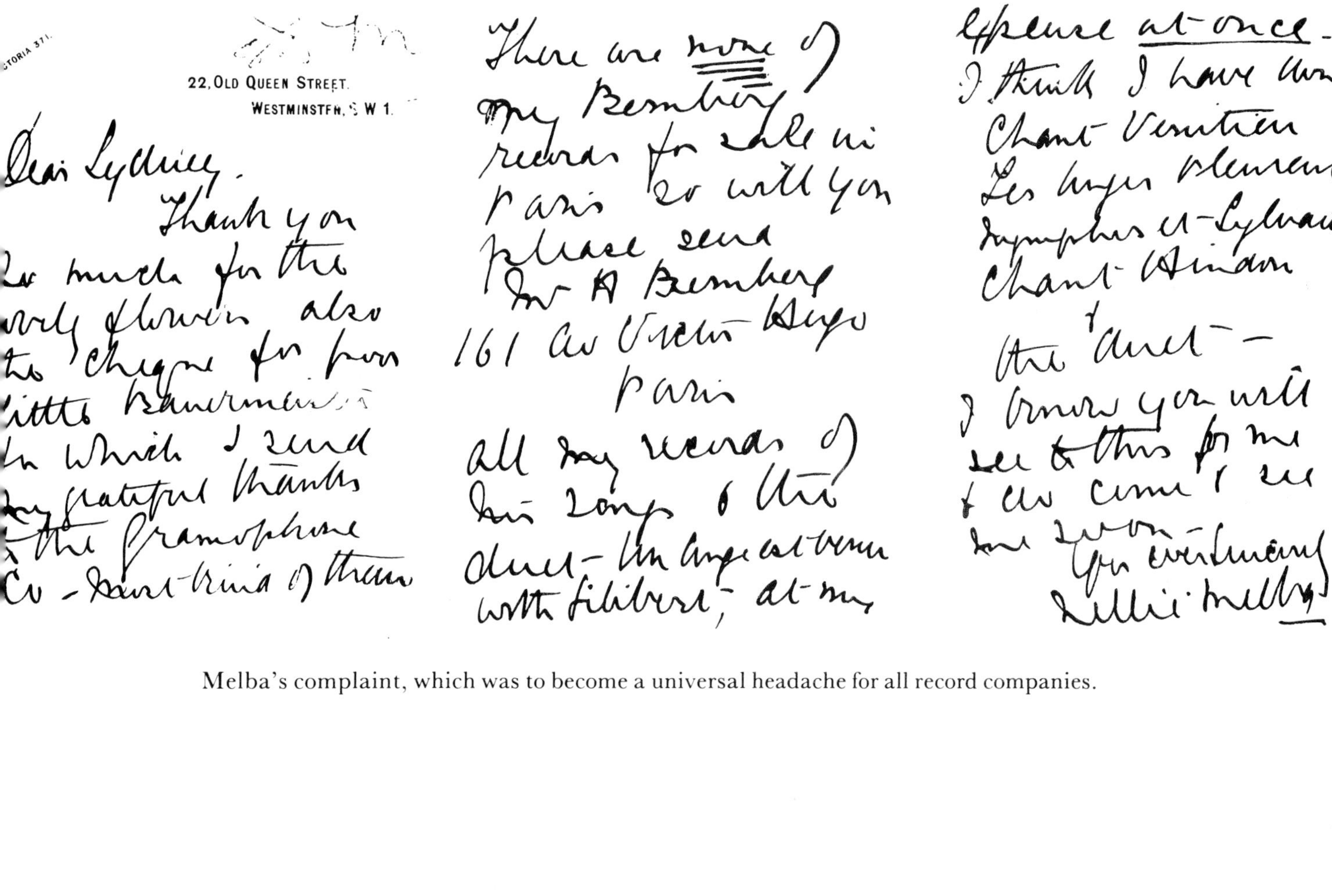

22, OLD QUEEN STREET.
WESTMINSTER, S.W.1.

Dear Sydney.
Thank you so much for the lovely flowers also the cheque for poor little Bauermeister in which I send my grateful thanks to the Gramophone Co - Don't think of them

There are none of my Bemberg records for sale in Paris so will you please send Mr H Bemberg 161 Av Victor Hugo Paris all my records of his songs & the duet - Un Ange est venu with Gilibert, at my expense at once - I think I have done Chant Venitien Les Anges pleurent Nymphes et Sylvains Chant Hindou & the duet - I know you will see to this for me & do come & see me soon - Yours ever sincerely Nellie Melba

Melba's complaint, which was to become a universal headache for all record companies.

Adelina Patti as Lady Harriet in Flotow's *Martha*.

PATTI

The last great artist to hold out against recording for the gramophone was the legendary Adelina Patti. By 1905 she was over sixty years old and living as something of a recluse at Craig-y-Nos, her castle in Wales, but reports indicated that her voice was still as pure and as beautiful as ever.

Madame Patti was universally recognized as the world's greatest soprano during the second half of the nineteenth century. When she was only twenty-five, Rossini had re-written the role of Rosina for her. She had triumphed at every major opera house. For one gala performance of *La Traviata* at Covent Garden it was said that Patti had worn jewels worth £20,000, and the cream of London society had jostled to get on stage and mingle with performers in the famous ballroom scene.

Until 1905, Patti rebuffed all approaches from The Gramophone Company. But the executives refused to give up. When she visited London, they sent a gramophone round to her hotel with a selection of the latest records. After listening to them, the great lady gave the first faint hope of a change of heart. She let it be known that she would consider recording only if she could be entirely satisfied with the outcome. The Company should negotiate with her solicitor, Sir George Lewis. She would go along with whatever he advised.

The conditions laid down by Sir George were straightforward enough: the entire recording apparatus was to be taken to Craig-y-Nos and made ready for immediate use. The operators were to wait there from day to day until Madame Patti indicated that she was willing to sing. After their experiences with Melba, The Gramophone Company directors made light of these terms. Fred and Will Gaisberg were sent off almost immediately, followed a few days later by Landon Ronald. All three were warmly received at Craig-y-Nos, and the recording equipment was set up in the castle's music-room. Patti showed considerable interest in what was going on, but precious little interest in singing. As the days passed, the Gaisbergs began to doubt whether the Diva would ever consider herself sufficiently 'in voice' to trust her talents to the recording machine.

Then Landon Ronald finally got things moving. One evening, after dinner, he sat down at the piano and played some of Patti's favourite selections. After a while she was persuaded to sing. Everyone in the room declared themselves overwhelmed by her artistry, and their enthusiasm convinced her that she would be able to record next day.

Ronald described the scene next morning. 'Her first selection was Mozart's "Voi che sapete", ' he wrote. 'She was very nervous but made no fuss and was gracious and charming to everyone. When she had finished her first record, she begged to be allowed to hear it at once. This meant that the master record would be unable to be used afterwards, but as she promised to sing it again, her wish was immediately granted. I shall never forget the scene. She had never heard her own voice and when the little trumpet gave forth the beautiful tones, she went into ecstasies! She threw kisses into the trumpet and kept on saying, "Ah, *mon Dieu!* Now I understand why I am Patti. Oh yes. What a voice! What an artist! I fully understand it all." Her enthusiasm was so naïve and genuine that the fact that she was praising her own voice seemed to us all to be right and proper.'

The rest of the session went off without a hitch, except when the luckless Fred Gaisberg tried to pull the singer back from the recording horn as she reached a particularly high note. Patti was, he recalled, 'most indignant – but later when she heard the lovely records she showed her joy just like a little child and forgave my impertinence'. The session produced fourteen records suitable for release. They were issued with a huge publicity campaign in February 1906. Patti, of course, had to have her own coloured label, too – it was pink – and her records sold, like Tamagno's, at one pound each. Advertisements were placed in two hundred British newspapers, and record shops festooned their windows with long streamers declaring: 'Patti Is Singing Here Today'.

Sun Life Assurance Society

CAPITAL £1,000,000   ESTD 1810   ISSUED £480,000

No. 126932

Chief Office
63, THREADNEEDLE STREET,
LONDON, E.C.

Temporary Assurance.

Whereas the SUN LIFE ASSURANCE SOCIETY (hereinafter called the Society) has received a proposal and declaration which are agreed to form the basis of this Contract **and whereas** on the date of the commencement of this Assurance a ~~first~~ ——Single—— premium was paid to the Society by the person to whom this Assurance is granted

Now know all Men by these Presents that ~~provided the Society receive the premium as set out in the Schedule underwritten~~ the Society will, on due proof given of the occurrence of the Event described in the Schedule, ~~of the Age of the Life Assured~~, and of title, pay to the person to whom this Assurance is granted or his (or her) executors administrators or assigns the Sum Assured together with such Bonus, if any, as may be due in accordance with the provisions of the Sun Life Assurance Act 1889 and the Laws and Regulations made pursuant thereto.

Schedule.

Date of the Commencement of this Assurance	28th November 1905.
Person to whom this Assurance is granted	THE GRAMOPHONE AND TYPEWRITER LIMITED whose registered Office is at No.21,City Road,London,E.C.,
Life Assured	THE BARONESS CEDERSTROM professionally known as MADAME ADELINA PATTI, Vocalist.
Sum Assured	ONE THOUSAND POUNDS.
Payable	in the Event of the death of the Life Assured on or before the 31st December 1905.
With or Without Participation in Profits	Without.
Premium .(Single)	Ten Pounds.
~~Payable~~	~~on~~ ~~and on the expiration of every succeeding calendar months thereafter until the death of the Life Assured~~
Date of Signature of this Policy	4th December 1905.

The Society's Assurance Fund Annuity Fund and Proprietors' Fund as well as the whole amount of the Society's uncalled Capital are, in accordance with the provisions of the Sun Life Assurance Act 1889 and the Laws and Regulations of the Society, the Funds liable to pay and make good any Claim in respect of this Assurance and it is hereby expressly agreed and declared that no Manager signing this Policy nor any other Proprietor shall be liable to any claim in respect thereof beyond the amount unpaid on the Shares held by him in the Capital of the Society.

In Witness whereof Two of the Managers of the Society have hereunto set their hands the day and year last mentioned in the Schedule.

Exd. Entd.

R. B. Salmon *Actuary.*

SPECIAL ADVANTAGES.

World Wide Assurance.—Occupation.—The Life Assured may reside in any part of the world and follow any occupation.

Receipts for Premiums.—For the protection of Policy-holders all Receipts for Premiums are issued on the Society's Printed Forms and signed by a principal Officer of the Society.

~~**Surrender Value.**—This Policy will acquire a Surrender value as soon as three full years' Premiums have been paid, the amount of such value will be quoted on application before expiry of the days of grace. (See Protection against Forfeiture.)~~

~~**Paid-up Policy.**—On application within the days of grace, a fully-paid up Assurance will be granted in lieu of the Surrender value.~~

~~**Loans** on this Policy, within its Surrender value, may be obtained by the absolute owner thereof.~~

Days of Grace.—Protection against Forfeiture.—Thirty days of grace are allowed for the payment of Annual, Half-yearly and Quarterly renewal premiums and ten days for Monthly renewal premiums. During the days of grace the Assurance remains valid, subject, in the event of death, to deduction of any overdue premium. In case of non-payment within the days of grace of any premium in respect of a Policy having a Surrender value such Policy will not lapse, but will be kept in force for One Year from the day on which the Premium became due. The overdue Premium with interest at the rate of Five per cent. per annum from the due date will be accepted at any time during the year, without evidence of health; a minimum charge of One Shilling will be made when the interest does not exceed that amount. At the expiration of a year, as before-mentioned, the then Surrender value, after deducting Premium and interest, will be applied to convert the Assurance into a paid-up Assurance without participation in future profits, provided the Policy be presented at the Chief Office for endorsement within the following thirty days.

Policies which have not acquired a Surrender value may generally be revived on production of evidence, satisfactory to the Society, as to the continued good health of the Life Assured and payment of arrears of Premium and interest at the rate of Five per cent. per annum from the due date, subject to a minimum charge of One Shilling as above.

Bonuses.—Valuations are made quinquennially. Participating assurances which have been in force upwards of two years at the date of a Valuation are eligible to rank for Bonus. In the event of a participating Policy producing a claim, after it shall have been five years in force, an Interim Bonus will be paid for each completed year of Assurance since the date of the preceding Valuation, or, if the Policy had not previously participated, since the commencement of the assurance; provided that if Bonuses are payable only on the Life Assured surviving a specified term of years, no Interim Bonus shall be paid unless the term shall have been survived.

The Gramophone & Typewriter Limited protected itself against Madame Patti's death prior to her completion of recording commitments in December 1905. This procedure became standard practice for all record companies dealing with stars and large advances.

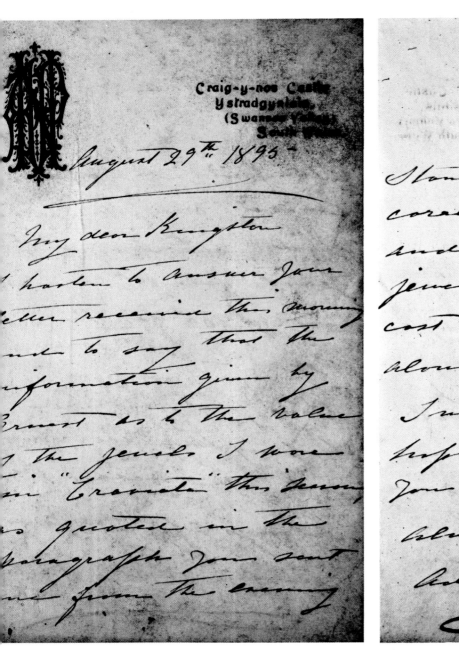

Letter to Mr Kingston.

Craig-y-Nos, Patti's castle in Wales, where she lived in virtual seclusion.

A regal Adelina Patti signs over a picture to Fred Gaisberg, on completing her recordings.

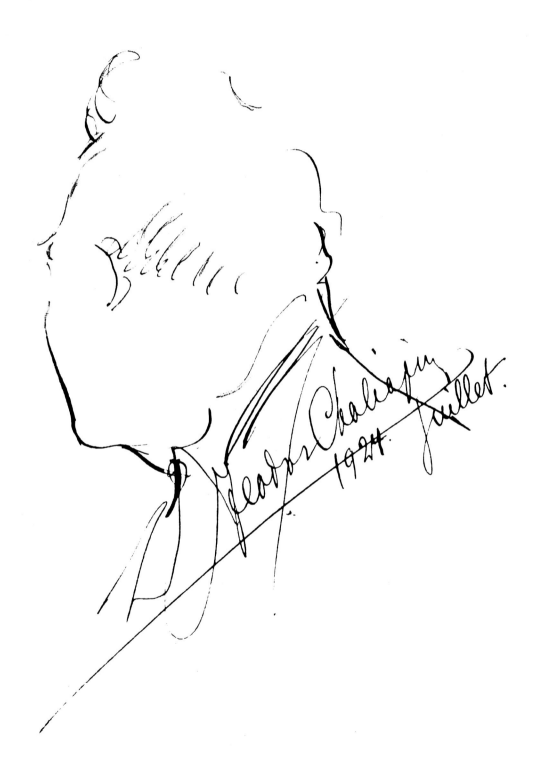

Self-caricature by Feodor Chaliapin, drawn in the Gramophone Company's visitors' book.

CHALIAPIN

Feodor Chaliapin was one of the first great opera stars to record for The Gramophone Company; his first, five-year contract, signed in 1907, was replaced by a new contract in 1910. When agreement was at last reached, the singer whisked Fred Gaisberg off to a party at Yar's Restaurant in Moscow. There, accompanied by cronies from the chorus, they spent the entire night singing Russian and gypsy songs. It was typical of Chaliapin. He was a giant of a man: lovable, generous, warm-hearted and endlessly infuriating.

Gaisberg wrote reams about the frustrations of trying to record him, but his memories were always tinged with affection. 'Chaliapin never made a gramophone record willingly,' Gaisberg recalled. 'He had to be coerced and almost kidnapped. He went to the grave without discovering the most propitious hour of the twenty-four in which to record. No law of punctuality was valid where Chaliapin was concerned: it was the duty of the world to wait for him. When I explained this to my directors, they would wax indignant and say they would not tolerate such behaviour. I would have to tell them that the Opera often waited, and even Grand Dukes thought nothing of it.

'Eventually I learned that it was useless to call a Chaliapin session before eight in the evening or even later. Before that time his big voice was not tuned up. To assemble musicians and Chaliapin before that time meant they would get on each other's nerves as he tried to warm up his voice with coughs, grunts, scales and squeals. Sometimes this wound up in a free fight for all.' The last twenty minutes of a session were usually the most productive, Gaisberg noted. By then, conductor and instrumentalists had been 'tamed to zero', and Chaliapin had sandpapered his voice to a flexible, velvet tone.

'It usually fell to my lot to fetch him to the studio,' the record-maker continued. 'If in good voice, this was an easy matter, but if he was dissatisfied with the condition of it, on arriving at his palatial home one usually found him sulking in bed. He would let out a roar at frequent intervals with the idea of proving that he could not possibly be expected to record; then, perhaps clearing his throat, he would call for a laryngoscope and his unfortunate valet had to hold up a mirror whilst he examined his vocal cords for red spots. Other times, when a study of his vocal cords revealed no red spots, we all breathed a sigh of relief; Chaliapin would then sing and if the song came forth smooth, rich and velvety he would smile, while we almost danced with joy and then rushed to get him dressed.

'His first recording session is an unforgettable memory. We persuaded him to enter a waiting sleigh, and when he reached the recording room he was greeted boisterously by the choir and orchestra, who had been waiting patiently for some hours. On that particular evening he was tireless. He continued in excellent voice for hours and we worked on one record after another until one o'clock in the morning. His pleasure was so great that he invited the choir and myself to finish the evening at the Strielka Restaurant, listening to its gypsy choir. This entailed hiring six sleighs and undertaking an hour's journey over hard frozen snow, through the biting Russian night winds.

'On arriving at the Strielka, we were received with a great welcome and the show began all over again with Chaliapin standing in the midst of the performers, singing and conducting combined choirs of the nomadic gypsies and members of the Opera House chorus who had come with us. Several hours passed in hilarious music-making, and Chaliapin was truly in his element. Trouble was occasioned by a certain Prince, who, being more than a little tipsy, became annoyed when our combined choir overwhelmed the efforts of an impromptu choir he had organized. There were hot arguments and bitter words and the hostess had difficulty maintaining peace.

'Eventually we returned to our hotels, completely exhausted by one of the most riotous nights I personally have ever witnessed, at about eight o'clock in the morning – not at all an unusual thing in the Russia of pre-War days.'

Gaisberg's family snaps of Chaliapin and family. At left in St Jean de Luc with stepdaughter
Stella and at right with grandchild and sealyham terrier.

Feodor Chaliapin, the Russian bass whose magnificent voice, towering stature and virtuoso
acting ability made him a legend in his own time. Chaliapin's greatest characterization, that of
Mussorgsky's Boris Godunov, is vividly preserved on various HMV recordings, especially those
made live at Covent Garden. Chaliapin also made many outstanding records of Russian songs
including the famous 'Song of the Volga Boatmen' and Mussorgsky's 'Song of the Flea'.

Chaliapin as Boris Godunov

A GROUP — CHALIAPIN, GORKI, H. G. WELLS, AND OTHERS

As Don Quixote

TETRAZZINI

It was a cold, foggy November night in 1907. Covent Garden Opera House was only half full. It had been a generally dull season and no one in England had heard of the singer making her debut that evening. Her name was Luisa Tetrazzini.

Harry Higgins, the managing director of Covent Garden, stood unhappily at the back of the house before the curtain rose, counting the empty seats. He had wanted to call the performance off. The conductor, Cleofonte Campanini, had told him about this new soprano and persuaded him to sign her for ten performances at the Garden, but the ink was barely dry on the contract before Higgins changed his mind and offered Tetrazzini £300 to cancel the agreement. She indignantly refused and threatened to drag Higgins through the courts unless he honoured the deal.

That November evening, waiting for *La Traviata* to begin, Higgins perhaps wished he had brazened it out. But then Tetrazzini made her entrance as Violetta and began to sing. The effect was electrifying. No one in the opera house was prepared for such a beautiful voice, for such breadth and purity of tone. Higgins later described it as the kind of voice he had dreamed all his life that he might one day hear. He waited just long enough to listen to the first brilliant cadenza, then rushed to his office to telephone the Fleet Street newspapers.

Music critics began to arrive one by one during the performance. At the end, the house rose to its feet and cheered for curtain-call after curtain-call. Poor Higgins had already started to worry about how Melba, then reigning prima donna at the Garden, would react. Next morning, the Sunday newspapers were full of the brilliant new discovery. The name Tetrazzini was on every front page, along with lyrical descriptions of her stunning debut success. On Monday, a representative from The Gramophone Company called at the Savoy with a blank cheque in his pocket and a recording contract for Madame Tetrazzini to sign. A message from the prima donna's suite advised him to wait. He waited. An hour passed. He asked if the lady could be reminded that he was waiting. She was. He was told to wait once more.

Tetrazzini was exacting delicious revenge. When she had first signed a contract with Covent Garden, the Company had cabled Carlo Sabajno, its maestro in Milan, to secure the lady for recording. Sabajno fixed an appointment to see her and arrived at her apartment on time, hat in hand, only to be told by the maid that Madame Tetrazzini was still occupied with her toilet. This was too much for the conductor. Loudly announcing that he had no intention of waiting about like a lackey, he stormed out, slamming the apartment door behind him. The maid reported his exit to her mistress, who was furious. She vowed she would get her own back on The Gramophone Company and, for the rest of her career, she refused to sing with an orchestra conducted by Sabajno.

When she thought the Gramophone Company representative had been kept waiting long enough at the Savoy, he was ushered into her suite. There was no question of negotiating a fee. The little Italian woman dictated her terms for recording and made it clear that there would be no discussion about them. She wanted 12,500 French francs to be paid at the start of each six months during a two-year contract. There would also be a royalty payment of five francs on the first 10,000 copies of each record sold, after which the royalty would be two and a half francs. After a month of worried consultations, the Company agreed to pay.

On 20 December 1907, nine days after the contract was signed, Tetrazzini arrived at the City Road studio to make her first record for the Company. By then she was a great star. Hundreds of people gathered outside the studio, hoping to catch a glimpse of her. Tetrazzini made twelve recordings during that session, then drove back to the Savoy in an open car, blowing kisses to the crowds lining the streets. Her relationship with The Gramophone Company was long and affectionate, despite its inauspicious beginnings. Tetrazzini laid the corner stone of the Company's huge cabinet factory at Hayes in January 1911 and visited the plant several times over the years to sing for the workers in the canteen. Her records were enormously successful and her version of Benedict's 'Carnival of Venice' was once described as 'perhaps the most wonderful record that has ever been made on a talking machine'.

Tetrazzini, at the cornerstone-laying ceremony at the Hayes factory in 1911, surrounded by silk- and bowler-hatted Gramophone Company executives.

Luisa Tetrazzini, the Italian soprano, had a coloratura voice of great beauty, range and security. She was also a skilled vocal actress and achieved international fame in a wide variety of roles. She died penniless, having earned a small fortune during her lifetime, and was buried at the state's expense. Her art lives on, however, in the many fine recordings she made for HMV.

Tetrazzini as Lakmé.

Reproduced by permission of The Haycock Cadle Co.

Hippodrome Revue
'HULLO TANGO!' RECORDS

vocal · instrumental · ragtime

FROM MUSIC-HALL TO WAR

The gramophone still had to compete with cylinder phonographs in the early years of the century. Indeed some people were convinced that the phonograph would be *the* music machine of the future. In America, 25-cent cylinders of popular songs, comedy sketches and recitations dominated the 'cracker-barrel trade'. In France, the Pathé factory near Paris was said to be turning out more than 1,000 phonographs and 50,000 cylinders every day. In Britain, a cheap phonograph outfit was peddled door-to-door around the country – for a guinea you could buy a player and six cylinders, usually the 'Liberty Bell' march, the 'Intermezzo' from *Cavalleria Rusticana*, a couple of hymns, 'Old Folks At Home', and a chorus song which was all the rage, 'Fol-de-rol-rol'.

One of the most successful British phonograph companies had been set up by two Americans – Louis Sterling, a dynamic young salesman from New York's lower East Side, and Russell Hunting, an ex-actor from Boston whose cylinder recitations under the name of 'Irishman Michael Casey' had sold in hundreds of thousands. Fred Gaisberg was an old friend of both men, and in the early days they often exchanged artists or new songs, believing that their markets were entirely separate. Co-operation ended abruptly, however, when Sterling decided that the days of the phonograph were numbered, and left the cylinder business to take over the flagging British branch of an American gramophone company, Columbia, which was having little success selling records made in the United States to British customers. When Sterling started recording in Britain, he quickly turned Columbia into The Gramophone Company's biggest and most aggressive rival.

In the undignified scramble for a dominating position in the popular song market, both companies happily poached each other's artists. Billy Williams, a popular Australian music-hall artist billed as 'The Man In The Velvet Suit', had given The Gramophone Company's HMV label a big boost with his hit 'When Father Papered The Parlour'. One day he showed up at the Columbia studio and offered to record the six new songs he had waxed for HMV a week earlier. Williams wanted only £40, so he could go to the races at Lincoln. Louis Sterling did not hesitate. He ushered the singer into the studio, then instructed the factory to give the pressing top priority. Within ten days, the new Billy Williams records were in the shops on the Columbia label – a full month before HMV's release date.

Nevertheless, The Gramophone Company was also capable of the occasional 'dirty trick' – even against its own artists. Harry Lauder, the famous Scottish music-hall star who recorded his entire repertoire for the Company, was furious when he discovered that another Scot called Hector Grant was releasing the same songs for Zonophone, the Company's cheap label . . . what he did not know was that Hector Grant did not exist. Peter Dawson, a young Australian baritone, was larking about after a recording session in the City Road studio one day when he suddenly delivered a perfect imitation of Lauder singing 'I Love A Lassie'. Fred Gaisberg asked him if he could do any more of Lauder's rollicking songs and Dawson said he could sing the lot. A few weeks later Hector Grant made his mysterious debut on Zonophone. The records were such a success that Hector was actually sent on a tour of public appearances, complete with kilt and sporran. Luckily, Peter Dawson was never recognized.

French catalogue 1910. This wonderful machine sold for FF137.50, roughly £11 sterling.

Years later, Peter Dawson, Harry Lauder and Fred Gaisberg met in a recording studio. Lauder suddenly turned to Gaisberg and said: 'Did ye no ken a chap by the name of Hector Grant? He had a grand voice.' Gaisberg decided the time had come to tell the truth. 'Surely you knew that Peter was Hector Grant?' he said quietly. 'Ye cannae tell me that,' Lauder scoffed. 'I saw Grant in Glasgow. He was a much older man.'

More patriotic songs sweep the country as war fever mounts.

Harry Tate, Violet Lorraine and Morris Harvey recording a patriotic song.

Smaller companies began to appear on the market, anxious to cash in on the growing demand for music. Some tried to combat their ingenious big brothers by introducing gimmicks. The Neophone label (which was to disappear in 1911) produced what it triumphantly described as 'indestructible' records made from papier mâché. Potential buyers were treated to a remarkable demonstration by a Neophone director, who hurled one of the new records out of a fourth-floor window, sent a small boy to retrieve it, then played it to the customers. Unfortunately, papier mâché records tended to curl up in direct sunlight.

Sales continued to rise, even though the price of two three-minute sides was around 2s 6d (equivalent to about £3 in today's money). Not everyone was convinced that the craving for recorded sound was a good thing. When a court at Stratford heard that a man had stolen a horse worth £16, and sold it for £4 to buy a gramophone, the judge declared that his use of the money 'was certainly evidence of weak intellect'. But such prejudice was becoming rare. Ballads, marches, music-hall turns, banjo and handbell solos all found a ready market, and the rival companies were constantly hunting for fresh sources of repertoire to satisfy the growing hunger for home entertainment.

After the sensational debut of Lehar's *Merry Widow* at Daly's Theatre in 1907, Columbia scored a number of notable successes with original cast recordings of London stage shows. Columbia representatives were present at every opening night, with flowers, champagne and a contract. Then Louis Sterling had the brilliant idea of sending scouts to the big seaside resorts at the beginning of the summer season. He rightly reckoned that the songs holidaymakers heard at end-of-the-pier shows would be the ones they would want to buy on record when they got home. Columbia men sat in on the shows at Blackpool, Southend and Douglas, wherever the big stars were appearing, and carefully noted the numbers that received the biggest reaction from the audience. Within weeks, the songs were in the Columbia catalogue.

The Gramophone Company hit back with a deal which put even the inventive Sterling in the shade. In an internal agreement to stop unnecessary competition between the two allied companies, it literally divided up the world in an agreement with the Victor Talking Machine Company of Camden, New Jersey, doubling the selection of records each could offer. The plan was beautifully simple. Two lines were drawn down a copy of Stanford's Library Map of The World. One followed longitude 30°W through the Atlantic Ocean, with a bend at the top to take in Greenland. The other ran along 170°W in the Pacific Ocean, with a large loop to embrace China, Japan and the Philippines. The area between these two lines, which included the USA, Canada and South America, was coloured red and 'given' to Victor. The rest – Europe, Africa, India, Russia, Australia – was coloured green and 'given' to The Gramophone Company. Within its own territory, each company was now free to trade without competition from the other. And in return for a small pressing-fee, each company was able to sell the other's records. It meant that the biggest record companies on either side of the Atlantic were now working together. Between them, they dominated the world.

So many records were now being made in Britain that The Gramophone Company's factory in Hanover could no longer cope. The system of sending master discs to Germany for processing had become hopelessly inefficient. In 1906 the Company bought a fifty-acre site at Hayes, Middlesex, and started building a huge new factory. Nellie Melba laid the foundation stone in May 1907, and the first record came off the presses in June 1908. By August, twenty-eight presses were turning out nearly 30,000 records every month.

The gramophone was now rapidly becoming an accepted part of everyday twentieth-century life. In 1909, the explorer Ernest Shackleton took one with him on his expedition to the South Pole. When the horn was lost – it slipped through a crack in the ice – a new one was improvised from an old piece of tin sheet, and worked perfectly. On his return, Shackleton reported that the gramophone had provided his men with their 'chief joy' during many months of gloom. To show his appreciation, he visited The Gramophone Company's City Road studio to make a record describing the difficulties they had overcome. Called 'Dash For The South Pole' it featured for several years in the Company's catalogue. A year later, the men accompanying Captain Scott on his tragic trek to the South Pole also took a gramophone along to keep them company.

In 1908, the first 'hornless' gramophones appeared in the shops. They were not particularly efficient, but the new 'speaker in a cabinet' was more socially acceptable to

More patriotic songs sweep the country as war fever mounts.

A bombed London after a
Zeppelin attack.

Recruiting office at Trafalgar
Square.

The British Expeditionary Force
listens to the gramophone in
Givenchy, France, in 1914. The
machine proved to be a great
morale booster.

The Marching Anthem on the Battlefields of Europe.

THE IMMORTAL

It's a Long, Long Way to Tipperary.

Written and Composed BY

JACK JUDGE AND HARRY WILLIAMS.

PHOTO BY LAFAYETTE.

Sung by THE SOLDIERS OF THE KING.

COPYRIGHT

LONDON,

Price 1/6 nett cash.

B. FELDMAN & Cᵒ 2 & 3, ARTHUR STREET, NEW OXFORD STREET, W.C.

Copyright MCMXII in America by B.Feldman & Cᵒ

'people of refinement'. They still considered the horn, no matter how it was embellished, as an ugly, vulgar thing, too unsightly for fashionable homes.

In August 1914, Europe was plunged into war. Much of The Gramophone Company's huge factory at Hayes was turned over to munitions, producing time-fuses, shell cases and aircraft parts. But records were still being pressed, and demand actually increased as a wave of patriotic fervour gripped the country. Songwriters responded with hits such as 'Pack Up Your Troubles', 'Roses Of Picardy', and 'Your King And Country Need You'. George Robey and Violet Lorraine recorded 'If You Were The Only Girl In The World', the show-stopper from a 1916 Alhambra revue called *The Bing Boys Are Here*, and it became one of Columbia's best-sellers. Peter Dawson changed his name again – to Will Strong – and waxed 'The Tank That Broke The Ranks At Picardy' for Zonophone. At the London Palladium, the wartime revue *Business As Usual* was playing to packed houses, and both The Gramophone Company and Columbia issued the show's hit numbers, songs with such stirring titles as 'When We've Wound Up The Watch On The Rhine'.

All the companies supported their patriotic songs with novelty records and miniature plays. 'With The Fleet In Action Off Heligoland' re-created, in just three minutes, the alarm, the German attack, the sinking of enemy ships, the rescue of survivors, rousing cheers and a final chorus of 'Rule Britannia'. Monologues like 'King Albert's Reply To The Kaiser' were popular, as were comedy sketches such as 'Building A Chicken House' by Will Evans. Music-hall comedian Charlie Penrose brightened the gloomy years by recording 'The Laughing Policeman'. It was such a hit that he devoted the rest of his career – it lasted until 1949 – to making laughing records for The Gramophone Company. They fill pages and pages of the catalogue – 'The Laughing Monk'. . . 'Widow' . . . 'Curate' . . . 'Bachelor' . . . 'Major' . . . 'Ploughboy' . . . 'Irish Girl' . . .

In 1918 Will Gaisberg transported his equipment to the front in Flanders and recorded a gas-shell bombardment. It was one of the first outside documentary recordings ever made and provided a vivid impression of what war was really like in an age before radio or television. Fred Gaisberg's contribution to the war effort was equally original. With an army escort, he toured prison camps to record the dances and folk songs of many different nationalities held behind wire fences in Europe – Serbs, Croats, Jugoslavs, Hungarians and Czechs. He also persuaded them to record passionate appeals for their countrymen to surrender and lay down their arms. These records were rushed to the front line and played on the biggest gramophones available, in the hope of inducing men on the other side to desert.

Hundreds of gramophones were sent to the front to try to relieve the misery of troops in the trenches. They did much to help morale. One young officer wrote: 'As one goes up to the trench at night and passes the last battered house where the road ends and the communication trench begins, a crack in the mud-plastered wall reveals a candle on a biscuit tin and two or three weirdly-lit faces listening to the strains of the latest revue. And somehow the

ALEXANDER'S RAGTIME BAND

BY IRVING BERLIN

EMMA CARUS

TED SNYDER Co.
MUSIC PUBLISHERS
112 WEST 38 St NEW YORK

Irving Berlin in London

witching rhythm of a waltz refrain bringing memories of happier days in London has a strangely heartening effect on the laden men stumbling on the cracked trench boards. Once we played our gramophone on the parapet. Some enterprising Boche retaliated for the sake of the Fatherland's musical reputation with a solo on a mouth organ.'

In 1917, a new composer presented the world with a song which was to capture the hearts of all who heard it, and somehow typifies the spirit and the longings of all war-weary people. His name was Ivor Novello, and the song was called 'Keep The Home Fires Burning'. In the same year, Edward German's great naval ballad 'Have You Any News Of My Son Jack?' was recorded for Columbia by Clara Butt, with an orchestra conducted by Thomas Beecham. And in America, the great Caruso joined the war cause with a recording of 'Over There' for Victor.

Peace in Europe in 1918 left industry temporarily exhausted. Tens of thousands of men had failed to return from the trenches. The record business, like every other, could not resume full production straight away. In any case, demand for patriotic songs, the staple diet of popular record buyers since 1914, was falling away. Something new was needed to sustain interest in gramophones and records. Fortunately, that something was just round the corner. It was to produce the greatest boom in record sales that the music machine had ever seen. It was called jazz.

ГРАММОФОНЪ

КАТАЛОГЪ
КАВКАЗСКИХЪ и ПЕРСИДСКИХЪ ЗАПИСЕЙ
АКЦ. О-ВА ГРАММОФОНЪ

МОСКВА
Тверская № 26

POTTER.

Февраль 1909.

TRADE MARK

GRAMMOPHON

Published by Russian Branch 1909.

DEUTSCHE GRAMMOPHON & THE RUSSIANS

The 1914–18 war may have boosted record sales, but The Gramophone Company suffered enormous losses abroad. The complicated transfer of master recordings from its Hanover plant to Hayes had not been completed by the time hostilities began in August 1914, and the Company had to start frantic negotiation, through neutral intermediaries, to protect the priceless recordings of such stars as Caruso, Scotti and Melba. The greatest fear was that Germany would melt down the precious matrices to make arms and ammunition. At last a message arrived from Berlin. The Kaiser's government recognized the artistic value of the master recordings, and was prepared to ship them to a neutral country, if The Gramophone Company would immediately send an equal weight of copper to Germany. Such a transaction required the approval of the British government, and the deal was put to the Cabinet, but Lord Kitchener opposed it vigorously: the enemy might hesitate to melt down such valuable objects as the matrices, whereas a consignment of bulk copper would immediately

◄The Russian catalogue of 1909 features Armenian, Circassian and Persian Tartars while the back page (above) features a peasant listening to 'His Masters Voice'.

Trevor William's share certificate in Deutsche Grammophon.

German catalogue.

The entire Deutsche Grammophon staff in Hanover in 1898.

The staff of the Russian branch around 1903.

Langersehnte Freude!

be used for munitions. Permission for the exchange was refused. The German government quickly confiscated the Hanover plant and its entire contents.

Even more disastrous blows were to come in Russia. The Gramophone Company had built a modern factory at the Baltic port of Riga to supply records to Central Europe, Scandinavia and the Balkan States. Its 120 presses were capable of producing 500,000 records every month for the booming Russian market. In the summer of 1915, when the Germans threatened to overrun the town, the Riga factory had to be abandoned. Some of the machinery and 10,000 master recordings were shipped to Petrograd, in the hope that production could be resumed. But a chronic shortage of fuel and the threat of new German advances forced a further withdrawal to Moscow.

By December, ten presses had been installed in a makeshift factory in the Russian capital and production began again, despite the difficult conditions. Then in November 1917, the Bolsheviks occupied Moscow and closed down all factories making luxury goods. Ohsoling, The Gramophone Company's manager, dismantled much of the equipment and draped the rest with grain sacks, to make the plant look like a warehouse and perhaps prevent it from being requisitioned. He maintained the lowest possible profile until he was ordered to appear before a Bolshevik tribunal, at which he was 'invited' to open up the factory and press propaganda records of speeches by Lenin and Trotsky. 'I could not answer with a direct "No", as I should have risked being shot,' Ohsoling later reported to London. Under the circumstances, he did the sensible thing and disappeared.

Elsewhere in Russia, the Company's British employees were getting out. Last to leave was Frederick Tyler, branch manager in Tiflis. Under threat of being called up for military service and sent to the Caucasian front, he sold whatever he could and caught the last train out of the city, eventually making his way back to England.

The Gramophone Company wrote off its Russian losses, but attempted to reclaim its property in Hanover and begin business again in Germany once the Armistice was signed. To the utter astonishment of the London directors, the Peace Treaty terms decreed that their German branch should remain in German ownership, and that they should be compensated for its loss. The new independent German company *Deutsche Grammophon Gesellschaft* – now known as Polydor International – not only retained the HMV "Nipper" trademark in Germany but also began issuing bargain-price records pressed from Gramophone Company matrices left behind in 1914.

A complicated twelve-year legal wrangle began, with The Gramophone Company trying to regain its trademark, if nothing else. But it was no good. 'We were completely baffled in our desire to get back what had been taken from us by an enemy we had defeated,' Alfred Clark noted with disgust. It was 1926 before The Gramophone Company regained a foothold in Germany with a new company, Electrola. The 'Nipper' trademark was finally purchased back by The Gramophone Company .

In the early days Royal speeches and occasions were assiduously recorded and marketed at a profitable margin. But British Royalty resisted the record until 1923, when a ten-inch record by George V and Queen Mary sold 77,000 copies throughout the world.

Royal records were listed separately in the catalogue thereafter and when they stopped selling were recorded for posterity. Each Royal recording artist was presented with his or her own microphone, some of which were crafted out of marble and precious metals.

ROYALTY
EMBRACES THE RECORD

From its earliest days, The Gramophone Company was quick to seize every opportunity of putting the voices of kings and queens on disc. Royal records bolstered prestige, and were avidly sought after. During its first forty years, the Company collected no less than seventeen royal warrants and recorded an exotic procession of kings, queens, sheikhs, sultans, maharajahs and caliphs. Undaunted by rebuffs at home – Queen Victoria was not amused by the gramophone, and her son, King Edward VII, heartily disliked it – the Company scoured the world for more co-operative royals.

In January 1903, the Queen of Rumania, a poet, read her work for the gramophone. She asked for the four records to be released under her pen-name of Carmen Sylva, with no mention being made of her regal status, but The Gramophone Company could not resist revelling in its triumph and added the words 'Queen Elizabeth of Rumania' under the pen-name.

In 1905, an enterprising Company agent called Maxim Pick wrote to the aged Shah of Persia, addressing his request to 'the Fountain of Light, the one who comprehendeth the Threshold of the August Presence, the Fortunate, the sublime, and the centre of happiness, may his Kingdom endure through the ages . . .' and begging, 'of the shining dust of your feet', for agreement to record Persian music. As an inducement to win sole rights for sale and distribution of the gramophone in Persia, Pick offered to give the Shah a new model every year, together with three hundred records. His Imperial Majesty graciously accepted the terms.

Pick was a salesman of rare ability. At the end of his recording tour of the country, in January 1906, he persuaded the Shah himself to record. Acoustic equipment was trundled into the Royal Palace and at least five records were made. Pick sacrificed two waxes by playing them back to the Shah immediately. This was a stroke of genius. The old man was so

1 9 3 5

"HIS MASTER'S VOICE"
RECORDS *for* FEBRUARY

THE KING'S
MESSAGE TO
THE EMPIRE
(page 2)

Portrait E.O. Hoppé

*Whatever kind of music issued in this monthly
Supplement appeals to you most strongly, do
not forget that the Catalogues of " His Master's
Voice " Records can guide you to a wealth of
examples*

"HIS MASTER'S VOICE"

impressed that, on the final record, he enthusiastically extolled the virtues of the gramophone, and its superiority over other talking machines. Thus, His Imperial Majesty Mouzaferedin Chan became one of The Gramophone Company's most exalted promoters. The records are now very rare indeed. The Shah became a great fan of the gramophone. Later that year, he asked Company representative F.W. Emmerson to bring some of the latest records to the Palace. One of them was the famous 'Laughing Song' by Henry Klauser, and Emmerson reported that the Shah laughed out loud when it was played. He added: 'The contortions on the faces of his people, who are not supposed to laugh in his presence, baffled description.'

Prince Nikolas (later to become King Nikolas I) and his son Mirko, and King Christian X of Denmark, were the next names added to the catalogue of regal recordings, but all efforts to persuade the British Royal Family to follow their example drew a blank. During the 1914–18 War, Princess Mary and Princess Alice often helped in the Church Army canteen set up at Hayes to feed munition workers who had taken over most of the factory. Volunteers to serve in the canteen were drawn from nearby towns on a rota basis, and the Windsor contingent frequently included young members of the Royal Family who were staying at Windsor Castle. Largely as a result of this link, the King and Queen paid a formal visit to the factory on 22 March, 1917.

'It was on this visit,' Alfred Clark recalled, 'that I first learned of the deep personal interest which King George V took in the gramophone. We had supplied a number of instruments and large quantities of records, but I did not realize that they were spread over his various homes at Balmoral, Windsor and Buckingham Palace, and that every day His Majesty found some time, if only for a few moments, to play his favourite music quietly in the solitude of his own room.'

Armed with this information, Clark stepped up his efforts to persuade the King to record for HMV. A tactful suggestion that His Majesty might make an appeal on behalf of some deserving charity met with no response. Then, early in 1923, the headmaster of a school near Hayes wrote to The Gramophone Company, asking if it would record a message from the King which could be played to children throughout the British colonies on Empire Day. Clark realized that if the Company put the idea forward, it would almost certainly be dismissed as a publicity stunt. So he suggested that the headmaster contact the Board of Education to press his case. The tactic worked. Sir Amherst Selby-Briggs, Permanent Secretary to the Board of Education, passed the request on to Lord Stamfordham, the King's private secretary, and when he put it forward, the King readily agreed to the plan.

On 27 March 1923, in a smoking-room at Buckingham Palace, both King George and Queen Mary recorded short speeches on one side of a ten-inch record. On the reverse side, the band of the Coldstream Guards played 'God Save The King' and 'Home Sweet Home'. William Manson, a Gramophone Company executive, carefully explained what the royal couple had to do. 'With a view to giving their Majesties some idea of the speed at which it

King Edward VIII visits Hayes in 1938.

King George VI inspects the Gramophone Company Home Guard at Hayes.

Princesses Elizabeth and Margaret recording a wartime message.

would be advisable for them to record, I made a record of the messages and played it over before the King and Queen made their record,' he noted. 'They listened most attentively to the various instructions which I gave them with regard to the technique of recording, and when the session was over they heard with very great interest some records by Caruso and Melba.'

Copies of the royal record, fastened with a special seal, were shipped to the far-flung corners of the Empire, and seal-breaking ceremonies were co-ordinated to invest the playing of the message with suitable importance. More than 77,000 copies were sold at 5s 6d each, and the £4,000 profit was donated to charities of their Majesties' choosing. The success of the venture led to a whole series of follow-up recordings, listed separately on the front page of the HMV catalogue under the heading 'The Royal Records'. They included a homily from the Prince of Wales on 'sportsmanship', a camp-fire chat from the Duke of York to be played at boys' camps throughout Britain, and virtually the entire Coronation service of George VI on a fourteen-disc set. There were also innumerable speeches from the opening of exhibitions or the launching of ships.

Elsewhere in Europe, King Alfonso XIII of Spain recorded a lecture on patriotism for the Spanish people at the Royal Palace in Madrid. Mussolini made a recording at Rome's Chigli Palace, after first forcing the Company's offer of a royalty up from five to ten per cent. Rumanian prime minister Jean Bratianu also recorded, and when he fell ill a few days later, Heinrich Conrad, the Company's general manager in Eastern Europe, rushed to his sickbed for a signature to authenticate the record . . . Bratianu died next day.

In August 1930, when the King of Rumania recorded for The Gramophone Company at his Sinaia summer palace, Conrad came up with an ingenious idea for ensuring that the disc was a best-seller. He had a sheet of vellum inserted into each sleeve, so that buyers of the record could write their own homages to the King. Purchasers were told that these sheets would be collected and bound into a 'Golden Book of the Nation', to be presented to Carol II. Naturally everyone wanted to be included in the book, and the record sold in incredible numbers. The King was so delighted with the sales and the book that he bestowed the Great Cordon of the Order of the Rumanian Crown on Alfred Clark. In return, the Company presented His Majesty with the latest electric gramophone.

In 1932, HMV recorded the British monarch's Christmas Day message from Buckingham Palace, a practice that has continued every year since. The discs never achieved large sales, and in later years the recordings have not been available to the public but continue to be recorded for posterity. Two copies of all the earlier royal records were bound in the finest leather and signed by the monarch; one is kept in the Royal Archives, the other is lodged in the EMI Music Archive at Hayes.

A RECORDING THEATRE IN A PALACE

THE above photograph shows H.M. the King of Spain making a gramophone record in one of the rooms of the Royal Palace, at Madrid.

This record consisted of two messages, one to the Spanish people and the other to the South American Republics, and the profits from the sale of this record will be handed over to H.M. the King of Spain for the purchase of comforts for the Spanish troops in Morocco.

The recording was carried out by the Spanish Gramophone Company, Limited ("His Master's Voice"), the manager of which, Mr. D'Arcy-Evans, is seen in the background.

Queen Mary of Rumania recorded her poetry for the gramophone, while King Alfonso XIII of Spain recorded messages to the Spanish people and the South American Republics, the proceeds of which were used to aid Spanish troops in Morocco.

121

LE HOT JAZZ

June 33   39

COMPAGNIE FRANÇAISE DU GRAMOPHONE
LA VOIX DE SON MAITRE
9 BOULEVARD HAUSSMANN 9 PARIS (9e)

THE DANCING YEARS

If, as one critic wrote, jazz arrived in America two hundred years ago in chains, it was at the turn of this century, in ghetto red-light districts such as Storyville in New Orleans, that it was set free. You could hear it on the streets as mourners returned from funerals to the strains of 'Oh Didn't He Ramble'. You could hear it in the crowded, smoke-filled dance-halls, and from the horse-drawn wagons that toured the town touting the next hop. You could hear it late into the night at bars and bawdy houses. And at dawn you could still hear it from cellars and cafés as the players jammed just for fun.

The young black musicians of the sprawling Mississippi Delta racial melting-pot had improvised an inspiring, intoxicating new style, weaving the syncopation of their ragtime and the emotional depth of their blues around tunes from the new nation's European heritage. They had run as kids beside white brass bands in street parades, then plundered pawnshops for second-hand trumpets, trombones and clarinets, converting the rousing Sousa marches they had heard into a music that satisfied their souls.

'They were bending the notes until they felt right,' wrote Rudi Blesh in his book *Combo USA*. 'Changing the brass tones until they sounded like the husky Sunday voices in the Holiness Church . . . moving the square march beat all round until it stopped marching and began skipping, running, leaping, dancing . . . letting jubilation and joy crowd out the martial aggressions of the white man's military music . . . creating a new music no one had ever heard before . . . making jazz.

'Without sheet music or the ability to read from it, the various instruments gathered like voices round the preacher, the high, strong, lordly trumpet or cornet. Over a syncopated roll of drums, the music simply began, like a conversation, each horn, clarinet, trombone adding to the story the trumpet was telling.'

The toe-tapping, romping, stomping style that emerged was irresistible, and the young pioneers were prepared to go to almost any lengths to join in. In 1900, fifteen-year-old

123

The Original Dixieland Jazz Band established the new music, Jazz, in England.

Ferdinand Joseph LeMenthe, later better known to the world as Jelly Roll Morton, was thrown out of the house by his grandmother when she discovered he was playing piano in a Storyville whorehouse. Louis Armstrong watched helplessly as his first marriage fell apart. He neglected his wife, he later recalled, because 'I was so crazy about the music, I couldn't think about much else'.

But for jazz to break out of the ghetto, it needed to be adopted by white musicians. Despite the Civil War and the emancipation of slaves, America, and particularly the South, was still riddled with race bigotry. Blacks were still called coons and niggers, confined to their own restaurants, hotels, washrooms and railway station platforms. The vast majority of white Americans dismissed their jazz as 'jungle music'. However, some were more enlightened and unable to ignore the heady exuberance of the new, lively rhythms. They heard the sounds of Storyville and the Barbary Coast, and began to re-create them on their own side of the tracks.

In December 1915, a Chicago nightclub owner came south for a New Orleans prize fight. In the Haymarket café, he listened nightly to a five-man white group playing jazz, and recognized their commercial potential. He offered them a ten-week contract at his Chicago club, and the band – Nick La Rocca on cornet, Leone Mello trombone, Alcide Nunez clarinet, Henry Ragas piano, and Johnny Stein drums, accepted. Billed as Stein's Jazz Band, they were an instant success in the windy city, and stayed for most of 1916. Then New York, the hub of America's entertainment industry, beckoned.

The famous Reisenweber Cabaret Café offered a trial residency, with the promise of $750 a week if the group were popular . . . They were not just popular, they were a sensation. Excited New Yorkers crowded into Reisenweber's every night to lap up the amazing new sounds of the quintet, who were now led by La Rocca and called the Original Dixieland Jazz Band. Damon Runyon, then a columnist for the Hearst group of newspapers, reported the 'importation from the west of a syncopated riot known as a jaz [*sic*] band'.

Maurice
CHICAGO

Recording companies, hungry to extend the popular music repertoire they had started to explore in 1909, were quick to pick up on the new style that was the talk of the town. Columbia offered La Rocca a trial recording session in January 1917, and he accepted eagerly. But the record makers insisted on the band making a jazz version of a standard popular tune as the main side. The session was not a success and Columbia lost interest.

Rivals Victor then stepped in, and agreed to let the band record what they liked. On 26 February, the Original Dixieland Jazz Band cut the first jazz record using two of their own tunes, 'Livery Stable Blues' and 'Jazz Band One-Step'. Two weeks later, the first pressings were on the streets. Within a month they were being played avidly on hand-cranked, spring-driven, unamplified gramophones right across America. More than a million copies were eventually sold.

In the ghettos of Kansas City, Oklahoma, Atlantic City, Baltimore and St Louis, the sound was familiar enough. But it was much more of a revelation in the white homes of the Midwest. In Davenport, Iowa, a young Bix Beiderbecke listened over and over again to the big 78 r.p.m. disc, and tried out the notes on his own cornet. In Chicago, a young Benny Goodman heard from his phonograph horn the style that was to be a major influence in shaping his career as the King of Swing nearly twenty years later.

Jelly Roll Morton

In those days, before radio and talking pictures, gramophone records were the trend-setters, the star-makers, the catalyst jazz needed to take the country – and later the world – by storm. But not everyone was convinced at first hearing. Alcide Nunez took the Original Dixieland Band to court, claiming he had co-written the melody of 'Livery Stable Blues' before quitting the band in Chicago. But on 12 October 1917 Judge Carpenter ruled that he was not entitled to copyright, because 'no living human being could listen to that result on the phonograph and discover anything musical in it'. But the Judge went on to admit grudgingly: 'There is a wonderful rhythm, something which will carry you along, especially if you are young and a dancer.'

There were enough young dancers around to make sure that that wonderful rhythm would be carried along. The New Orleans pioneers were starting to spread the message right across the States.

◄The immortal Duke Ellington, the earliest successful black recording artist and composer.　　127

McKinney's Cotton Pickers

Jelly Roll Morton had gone to California. Joe 'King' Oliver had taken his Creole Jazz Band to Chicago's teeming South Side, bequeathing his coveted place in the Kid Ory band to a youngster who, at sixteen, could 'swing like a garden gate' – Louis Armstrong. Another teenager, Sidney Bechet, had gone to New York with Freddie Keppard's Original Creole Orchestra. The nineteen-year-old wove his clarinet magic at the Winter Gardens some months before the Original Dixielanders hit town. 'No one knew what to do when they heard this music,' he recalled. 'They never heard anything like it in their lives; they didn't know if it was for dance, or sing, or listen.' A Victor talent-scout had, in fact, given Keppard the chance to make the first jazz record. The black leader refused adamantly; some said it was because he feared his music would be pirated by others if he committed it to wax. It was 1922 before the first black New Orleans band was captured on record – Kid Ory's Sunshine Band.

The spread of jazz from New Orleans was accelerated in November 1917. Storyville, the notorious 38-block red-light area set up in 1897 by city alderman Sidney Story with the aim of centralizing vice in one district, was closed down by order of the US armed forces after disturbances between navy men and civilians. The jazzmen, whose music had become as big a draw as the nubile girls in short skirts and red shoes, drifted north, and found plenty of clubs anxious to cash in on 'the authentic New Orleans sound'. Prohibition, introduced in 1920, gave the jazzmen another boost. Speakeasies flourished alongside the dance-halls of Chicago. At one time, it was estimated the city had 20,000, most of them offering live entertainment. What was good for the gangsters was great for jazz.

Louis Armstrong, nicknamed Satchelmouth or Dippermouth by his jazz colleagues, had gained his mastery of the trumpet in the local coloured reformatory, then progressed from Kid Ory's band to playing the New Orleans–St Louis paddle-steamers that cruised leisurely up and down the Mississippi. In 1922, King Oliver made a place for him in his Chicago band: their double solo slots, cornets soaring and dipping as if each could read the other's mind, were soon the talk of the South Side. Future generations of jazz giants – Beiderbecke, Gene Krupa, Jimmy McPartland, Davey Tough, Muggsy Spannier – flocked to watch them. Established bandleaders like Paul Whiteman and Paul Ash arrived with their arrangers to take notes on the music that would pep up their own performances.

RIALTO RIPPLES

Rag

By
GEORGE GERSHWIN
And
WILL DONALDSON

NEW YORK   JEROME H. REMICK & CO.   DETROIT

Savoy Orpheans recording for Pathetone.

The Black Bottom dance, all the rage in London.
Jazz party on a river boat, 1924.

The '20s were starting to roar, and recording companies were determined to cash in on the craze. White bands were OK, but it was the black bands which provided the real excitement. The problem was how to record them without offending the white sensibilities of some Southern states. The answer was to create cheap label 'race record' subsidiaries, featuring black artists and sold only in black districts. Columbia opened the Okeh Phonographic Corporation in Chicago, and in 1920 Mamie Smith became the first black singer to record jazz songs, waxing 'That Thing Called Love' and 'You Can't Keep A Good Man Down'. The success of the disc – it sold 75,000 copies in Harlem alone, the first month after issue – alerted the other companies to the commercial potential of coloured artists. Okeh quickly snapped up the best of the talent: Ma Rainey, Fats Waller, Louis Armstrong and Bessie Smith.

Unlike the classical singers of the early gramophone years, there was never any problem getting the jazzmen into the studio. They were only too ready to record – for anyone who asked them. Between March and November 1923, King Oliver's Creole Jazz Band made thirty-seven records on four labels, Gennett, Paramount, Okeh and Columbia.

Their eagerness was all the more surprising because of the problems caused by the primitive state of the recording process. Jimmy Durante, later to become a comedian but then a rag-style pianist with a New Orleans jazz band, said: 'We couldn't use drums in those days. The recording machine couldn't take the vibrations – it would send the needle off the record. Imagine recording a Dixieland outfit without drums! Just trumpet, clarinet, and trombone, with me supplying the rhythm section from piano.'

Layton and Johnston, the two black American singers who became
British recording stars.

Paul Whiteman and his band.

When King Oliver and Louis Armstrong first went into a studio, their powerful cornets ended up twenty feet from the giant recording horn that picked up the sounds – while the bell of Johnny Dodds' clarinet was practically inside it. Bill Johnson's booming string bass was out – it caused the same problems as did drums – and he had to play banjo, and drummer Baby Dodds could only use his snares and a woodblock.

Nor was the emasculated sound the only problem. There were no tapes to be spliced if a note was fluffed. Each recording still went on to a massive master disc, cut by a needle, and if anything went wrong the whole performance had to start again. Recording engineers lived on the frayed edges of their nerves.

Nevertheless, the artists were happy to record and were amazingly relaxed about it. 'We'd just make them things up as we went along,' Louis Armstrong recalled. 'Make 'em up in the studio . . . They wasn't as particular then as they was today.' Once, Satchmo invited friends he had been drinking with all night to a session at the Victor studio. The party included Jack Teagarden and drummer Kaiser Marshall, who recalled: 'We had been working the night before and the record date was for 8 a.m., so we didn't bother about going to bed; I rode the boys around in my car in the early morning hours, and we had breakfast about six. We took a gallon jug of whisky to the session. After we recorded a number, the studio man came round with his list to write down the usual information – composer, name of tune, and so on. He asked Louis what the tune was called and Louis said, "I don't know." Then he looked around and saw the empty jug sitting in the middle of the floor, and said, "Man, we sure knocked that jug – you can call it 'Knockin' A Jug'." And that's the name that went on the record.'

Legendary pianist Fats Waller, composer of 'Honeysuckle Rose' and 'Ain't Mis-behaving', was also casual about recording. He once missed two Okeh sessions, explaining: 'I must have overslept somewheres.' After he signed for Victor, the company found that it paid to collect him. If he was not asleep somewhere, he would still be going strong, barely sober, at a piano in one of the Harlem clubs. A taxi would rush him to Victor's studio in Camden, New Jersey, always carrying a quart of hundred-per-cent proof Old Grandad under the seat to sustain him through the session.

George Gershwin.

By 1925 the market was flooded with jazz records. Radio had just begun, and live broadcasters over the air whetted the appetite for permanent reminders of the fleeting magic. In Kansas City, the Benny Moten band was recording for Okeh with the man who would later lead it to international acclaim, pianist Count Basie. In New York Fletcher Henderson was setting jazz to big-band arrangements at the Roseland Ballroom and recording for Vocalion, while, at the Cotton Club, Edward Kennedy 'Duke' Ellington was starting his fifty-year career by making tracks for Perfect, Gennett, Vocalion and, later, Brunswick, Columbia's 35-cent label.

Paul Robeson

The multi-instrument, richer arrangements of leaders like Henderson and Ellington were building on the jazz combo base, and other big bands were developing along similar lines. In Harlem, the flappers flocked to the Savoy Ballroom to hear hunchback drummer Chick Webb and his singing discovery, Ella Fitzgerald. Out west, Paul Whiteman, the son of a music teacher, was using some of the techniques he had picked up as a violinist with the Denver Symphony Orchestra to provide a swinging, showy stage spectacular. He launched Bing Crosby as one of his Rhythm Boys, hired the first female big-band singer, Mildred Bailey, commissioned and premièred George Gershwin's *Rhapsody In Blue*, and took on star soloists like Bix Beiderbecke and the Dorsey brothers.

In the Midwest, Jean Goldkette was setting alight first Chicago, then Denver, with several top jazz bands. Apart from his own band, he controlled the Orange Blossoms, later to become the influential Casa Loma Orchestra, and McKinney's Cotton Pickers, whose hits for Victor included 'If I Could Be With You One Hour Tonight' and 'Baby Won't You Please Come Home'. Chicago drummer Ben Pollack led a star-studded line-up, first in California then at New York's Park Central Hotel, which included Glenn Miller, Jack Teagarden and Benny Goodman, who had joined the musicians' union aged only twelve.

Pollack joined the happy-go-lucky recording roundabout. Although signed to Victor on an 'exclusive' contract, his band did bootleg work for a variety of labels, playing under such fanciful titles as Whoopee Makers, Hotsy Totsy Gang, the Lumberjacks, Dixie Daisies, Mills Musical Clowns, and even the tongue-in-cheek Ben's Bad Boys. Another band, the California Ramblers, waived their royalties from Columbia so they could record for competitive labels under seventeen phoney names. Such antics drove the industry's executives to distraction. Once Sophie Tucker was in the middle of a session for Okeh when the studio door burst open and her manager rushed in, bawling: 'You can't record here, you've got an exclusive contract with Aeolian.'

But it was not all fun for the jazzmen. They had to fight against a colour prejudice that was to help destroy stars such as Billie Holiday and Lester Young. And they had to battle against a strong puritan streak which swept America in the '20s, showing itself most clearly in the prohibition of alcohol. In reactionary minds, jazz was inextricably linked with the bars, gambling dens and whorehouses that had given the music its start, and for many jazz became a symbol of crime, feeble-mindedness, insanity, sex and alcoholism. The *New York American* reported in January 1921: 'Moral disaster is coming to hundreds of young American girls through the pathological, nerve-irritating, sex-exciting music of jazz orchestras, according to the Illinois Vigilance Association. In Chicago alone, the association's representatives have traced the fall of 1,000 girls in the last two years to jazz music.' But despite its enemies jazz was everywhere: in cafés, cabarets, clubs, restaurants, ballrooms, silent-movie theatres, Broadway shows, on the radio airwaves and on the gramophone turntables. It was, of course, inevitable that jazz would cross the Atlantic.

Europe had imitated American dance developments since 1912, when the syncopated rhythm of ragtime was first heard. Irving Berlin's 'Alexander's Ragtime Band' took the country by storm, and when the ragtime revue *Everybody's Doing It*, also by Berlin, opened at the Empire in London's Leicester Square, the rival record companies almost came to blows in the race to be first out with a disc of the title-song. Then the American Ragtime Quartet came to London and made the first dance records for Columbia. Young Britons followed each new trend, and the two-step, turkey trot and grizzly bear tested the floorboards in every nightspot. Record sales soared as the nation's toes twinkled. The Gramophone Company sponsored tango demonstrations. Columbia replied with an instruction booklet with its first foxtrot record, 'Watch Your Step'.

Jazz arrived in Europe in 1919, brought by the band that made America's first jazz record. The Original Dixieland Jazz Band opened at the London Hippodrome on 7 April in a musical revue called *Joy Bells*. And since the audience included many US servicemen fresh from the battlefields of Europe, they received a tumultuous welcome. But their run in the show lasted just one night. Star comedy-singer George Robey, possibly worried by the rival attractions of a down-the-bill act, issued an ultimatum to producer Albert de Courtville: either they went or he did. They went.

The band moved to Rector's nightclub, a popular haunt for London's trendy flappers and their sleek, dinner-jacketed escorts. The customers loved the wild, exciting improvisations. A tour of variety theatres was followed by a stint at the newly opened Palais de Danse in Hammersmith, then by an engagement at the prestigious Embassy Club. Before returning to America in July 1920, the group recorded 'Tiger Rag' for Columbia. A startled reviewer said of the record: 'It is peculiarly insidious . . . it all comes out with such absolute spontaneity that it gets hold of you to an alarming extent.'

In June 1919 another American band came to England. Will Marion Cook's Southern

The young Louis Armstrong.

Syncopated Orchestra opened at the Royal Philharmonic Hall, Sidney Bechet on clarinet. In the audience sat Ernest Ansermet, the great classical conductor. His thoughts on what he saw and heard were later published in the magazine *Revue Romande*, and they proved that, even if jazz had to battle the Establishment in its homeland, it had influential friends across the Atlantic.

After noting the 'astonishing perfection, the superb taste and the fervour' of the orchestra's playing, Ansermet waxed lyrical over Bechet's solos. 'Their form was gripping, abrupt, harsh, with a brusque and pitiless ending like that of Bach's Brandenburg Concerto . . . what a moving thing it is to meet this very black, fat boy with white teeth and that narrow forehead, who is very glad that one likes what he does, but who can say nothing of his art, save that he follows his "own way".' To be compared to Bach, to be acclaimed for one's 'art', was more than any jazz musician back home could dream of.

For a few months, British bands tried desperately to emulate the sounds of the Original Dixielanders and the Southern Syncopators. Then, in 1920, a record arrived from America which was to change the whole direction of British popular music. 'Whispering', played by Paul Whiteman's dance band, was America's first million-selling disc and the first indication to European musicians that, with the advent of the saxophone, jazz could be successfully orchestrated.

The record was released in Britain by The Gramophone Company, now becoming better known as HMV. When the manager of the Queen's Hall Roof Orchestra heard an early pressing, he rushed it to Langham Place, where his band were rehearsing. The players listened to the disc in utter amazement, but only one of them, the relief pianist, realized that what they were hearing was 'orchestrated' jazz.

Young Jack Hylton had been a boy soprano, assistant pianist with a North Wales pierrot troupe, conductor to a touring pantomime and a cinema organist before joining the Queen's Hall Orchestra. Along the way he had learned to read music, unlike most of his new colleagues, and, that day at Langham Place, he alone understood that Whiteman's band was not improvising, but playing from a previously scored arrangement. Hylton offered to write something similar for Queen's, and was promptly made the band's permanent arranger.

All British recording companies were looking for a home-grown answer to the Whiteman sound, and when HMV heard Hylton's arrangements, they signed the orchestra for studio sessions. Each player was to receive a flat fee of £5 per recording. Hylton asked for an extra ten shillings (50p) for his arranging efforts and when that was rejected, he asked for a credit on the record labels instead. Since this cost nothing, HMV agreed. The records, made at Hayes, Middlesex, in May 1921, were released by The Queen's Dance Hall Orchestra, directed by Jack Hylton. Inside twelve months Hylton was so well known that he was able to set up his own band, recording 'Ain't Nobody's Darling' for HMV in 1922, and

Paul Robeson on the balcony in *Showboat*, Drury Lane Theatre, 1928

after stints at London nightspots like the Grafton Galleries, the Piccadilly Hotel and the Kit-Kat Club, he led his men on a top-of-the-bill tour of the nation's leading variety theatres.

Though Hylton occasionally described his musicians as a jazz band, and included some of Britain's most swinging sidemen – future band leaders Jack Jackson (trumpet) and Ted Heath (trombone) were just two – he seldom gave jazz free rein. Nevertheless, his records were the biggest sellers in the HMV roster for ten years. A staggering 3,180,000 Hylton discs were sold in 1929 alone.

The London hotels were quick to cash in on the new mania for dancing. They realized that resident bands and guest stars not only brought in customers but added prestige to the hotels themselves, particularly when, in 1923, the British Broadcasting Corporation started live transmissions from the major London venues. The Savoy in the Strand led the way with Bert Ralton's Savoy Havana Band and the Savoy Orpheans, led by Debroy Somers. Soon, radio listeners got hooked on the vicarious thrill of tuning in to a dream world, a night out in London's West End. The two Savoy bands joined Hylton as the highest-paid dance groups contracted to HMV during the '20s, and made more than three hundred records between 1922 and 1927, mainly waltzes, medleys from shows, and straight popular songs.

Their biggest rival was Bert Ambrose, leader of what was then regarded as the Rolls-Royce of dance bands, who was earning an astonishing £10,000 a year at the Mayfair Hotel with his smooth, melodic arrangements. Born in London, but taken to America as a youngster, Ambrose had tasted the big-band scene in New York before the owner of London's Embassy Club enticed him home in 1920. He began recording for Columbia in May 1923, but after he switched to the Mayfair Hotel in 1927 he transferred to HMV, the main label of The Gramophone Company. Dealers who won the right to stock HMV releases felt they had arrived at the pinnacle of their trade.

Ambrose had to compete for material with fellow HMV star, Jack Hylton, and such top American bands as Paul Whiteman, Jean Goldkette, George Olsen and Fred Waring, but there was no shortage of good popular tunes to be set to dance tempos. Cole Porter, George Gershwin and Irving Berlin were in their prime, and the musical stage offered a succession of hits – *The Desert Song, No No Nanette, Rose Marie, Showboat* – that provided rich pickings for orchestras.

Despite gloomy predictions that radio would kill the gramophone, record sales soared. HMV were producing more than seven and a half million discs a year at their Hayes plant alone. The staid *Gramophone* magazine, launched in April 1923, reported: 'Every month new and more exciting dance tunes are produced which, as they weary us, we discard for newer and still more exciting ones. . . . The gramophone is most convenient; no need to be careful of the life of the records, you can wear them out and get the latest.'

In July 1923, another *Gramophone* reviewer noted a further advantage of the turntable. 'To the gramophone dance record we owe one social improvement,' he wrote. 'The

REVISTA COLUMBIA

Josephine Baker EXCLUSIVA

"wallflower" in the dance room is disappearing. Young folk have the opportunity to practise at home to music supplied, via the gramophone, by first-class bands. Up to date and up to tempo, these records have killed the shyness that used to overtake the infrequent dancer on entering a ballroom.'

The influence of the gramophone was also spreading, thanks to a new portable version launched by HMV at the Ideal Home Exhibition at London's Olympia. 'Nearly every Turkish harem is now equipped with a gramophone,' The Gramophone Company's magazine, *The Voice*, reported incredulously. 'The Turk has found that no present gives so much pleasure to his favourite wife as this modern musical instrument, coupled with a selection of up-to-date records. It relieves the tedium of her life of enforced seclusion and is a link with the world without.' From Africa, HMV's representative reported after a tour of Zanzibar, Mauritius, South and East Africa: 'Dancing clubs for the white population exist everywhere, while invitation dances are also in great vogue. Nearly every household has a gramophone and a variety of HMV records.' Both the Sultan of Egypt and the 'dusky ruler' of Buganda were noted by *Voice* as being good customers. And when a party of Europeans was kidnapped by bandits in Morocco, the ransom demanded was £12,000 plus a gramophone and one hundred records. The hostages were released unharmed when HMV met the last two demands.

As sales boomed in Britain, competition between HMV and Columbia intensified, with each company shamelessly poaching artists from the other. HMV lured the Savoy Havana Band away from Columbia in 1924, then Columbia persuaded Paul Whiteman to leave HMV. The Savoy Orpheans, under contract to Columbia, were also moonlighting for HMV as the Romaine Orchestra and the Albany Band.

When Fred Astaire and his sister Adele came to London for the first time in 1923, they recorded two numbers from the hit show *Stop Flirting* for HMV. (One had the remarkable title, 'The Whichness Of The Whatness Of The Whereness Of The Who'.) By the time the couple returned to star in *Lady Be Good*, Columbia had signed them. At one session they recorded 'Fascinating Rhythm', with a young George Gershwin at the piano, plus the first ever tap-dancing record, 'The Half Of It Dearie Blues'.

The fact that an artist was under contract, or about to be signed by one company, made him or her all the more desirable to the other. When two black American singers, Turner Layton and Clarence Johnstone, made their cabaret debut at London's Café de Paris, Raymond Langley, chief artists' manager at Columbia, was in the audience and invited them over to his table after their act. When he asked if they would be interested in making records, the two explained that they had been invited to test at HMV the next day. 'Artists like you make a test!' scoffed Langley. 'It's absurd. We don't need to make any tests. I'll give you a contract right now.' And to the astonishment of the two young Americans, Langley scribbled out a contract on a Café de Paris menu, offering £100 per session plus five per cent royalties on each disc sold. At 2 a.m., over a bottle of champagne, Layton and Johnstone signed, and over the next ten years collected more than £100,000 in royalties from a string of hits which included 'It Ain't Gonna Rain No More', 'Bye Bye Blackbird', and 'Birth Of The Blues'.

In 1924 came a development that forced the two big recording rivals into a temporary and uneasy alliance. A team of engineers at the Bell Telephone laboratories in America invented a system of electrical recording. Apart from the restrictions it put on artists – huge funnels that picked up every sound, the jumpy needle that ruled out heavy bass or drumming – the acoustic recording procedure used by all early record companies had technical limitations for the listener. It could reproduce sounds only between the frequencies of 164 and 2,088 cycles, whereas the human ear could pick up sound between 30 and 15,000 cycles, so early gramophone records never had a really natural tone. Experiments to improve recording technique began in 1919, and by 1924 the Bell team, led by Joseph P. Maxfield, had produced an electrical system which could faithfully record a frequency range of 50 to 5,000 cycles.

Bell sent wax masters made by the new process to the Pathé laboratories in Brooklyn, New York, for processing. Unknown to them, a number of extra pressings were made, and these began to circulate in the trade. On Christmas Eve 1924, a couple of the pirate pressings reached Columbia boss Louis Sterling at his London home and ruined his Christmas. Sterling immediately realized that the greatly improved quality of electric recording would make acoustic discs worthless – and his company had just completed its most ambitious recording programme of symphonic works ever. Never a man to waste time, on 26 December he boarded a ship for New York to try to acquire the rights to the electrical recording process. When his parent company Columbia of America, proved reluctant to pursue a deal, Sterling raised $2½ million from a bank and bought the company out.

Electric recording gave music a depth and body it had never had on disc before. Bass notes and high-flying strings came through loud and clear. In addition, recording sessions were easier. Musicians no longer had to gather round the recording horn, but could spread themselves out in a roomy studio and play more naturally, confident that microphones were picking up their notes. Engineers could control the volume during recording, strengthening weak sound waves, reducing the blast of louder notes.

To avoid rendering every catalogue obsolete at a stroke, record companies tacitly agreed to keep the technical breakthrough a secret. In America, Columbia and Victor shared the patent with Western-Electric, but for a year no one knew. Both companies began re-recording their best-sellers with the new system, but the only clues on the label were a circled W on Columbia's discs, and the letters VE on Victor's.

In Britain too, Columbia and HMV agreed to sit on the news and, when the new records came out, they were described with every superlative in the book: astounding, sensational, amazing, etc. – without a mention of the new process. Music critic Ernest Newman of the *Sunday Times* was impressed. 'At last an orchestra really sounds like an

The great French recording stars of the '20s, Josephine Baker (previous page), Mistinguett and
her protegé Maurice Chevalier.

orchestra,' he wrote. 'We get from these records what we rarely had before – the physical delight of passionate music in a concert room or opera house.'

The uneasy alliance between Columbia and HMV did not last long. With their new improved product able to match the sound of radio, and with sales increasing again, the dirty tricks returned. Columbia sent an office boy to hang around the pubs where musicians gathered to try and find out which songs HMV had recorded recently. As The Gramophone Company was still run largely by committees and conducted business in a somewhat leisurely fashion, Columbia could often record a song long after HMV but rush it into the shops first. The HMV system had other drawbacks, too. In 1925 the Artists' Committee auditioned a young singer, then decided he was 'quite unsuitable for recording purposes'. Three years passed before Noël Coward was given a second chance, and his records stayed in the HMV catalogue for years, selling steadily. He recorded 'Mad Dogs And Englishmen' in 1932, and later advised 'Mrs Worthington' not to put her daughter on the stage.

The search for big-sellers extended to Europe in 1928 when Columbia bought control of Pathé Frères, the biggest recording company in France. On the books were three stars who dominated popular entertainment in Paris: Mistinguett, whose legs drove men wild; Maurice Chevalier, the man she had discovered as a red-nosed comic among the Left Bank cafés and turned into her comedy partner and lover; and the beautiful black American dancer Josephine Baker. Mistinguett had started making records before the 1914–18 war, but her biggest success came in 1920, when she recorded 'Mon Homme' and 'J'en Ai Marre'. The first song became her signature tune, and it came as a nasty surprise when she discovered on arrival in America in 1923 that it had been given English lyrics and recorded by Fanny Brice.

Chevalier had made his first recording with HMV in London and the song he put on wax rejoiced in the title 'On The Level You're A Little Devil But I'll Soon Make An Angel Of You'. In 1929 he too went to America, to star in a Hollywood musical, *Innocents of Paris*. The hit song from it, 'Louise', made him an international name.

Josephine Baker had crossed the Atlantic in the opposite direction to find fame. The stunning former chorus girl became the sensation of Paris when she danced at the Théâtre des Champs-Elysées wearing little more than a skirt of bananas. She began recording in 1926, and made a big impact with her version of 'La Petite Tonkinoise'.

At about the same time, another star was emerging in Germany. In 1928 two young girl-singers recorded a duet for Electrola in Berlin called 'Me And My Best Friend'. The lyrics were decidedly risqué, even for broad-minded Berliners, and one of the girls was later to deny vehemently that she had ever made the record; she insisted her career began in 1930 when she made a film called *The Blue Angel*. Her name was Marlene Dietrich.

The '20s had dazzled the record industry as they had dazzled the world. During the dancing decade, it seemed that there was no limit to public demand for discs. More and more homes were being supplied with electricity, and broadcasting, far from killing the record industry, had stimulated demand. Musical movies further boosted sales: spectacular films like *Broadway Melody* and *Hollywood Revue* followed the trend-setting *Jazz Singer*, and records from them sold in fabulous numbers.

HMV and Columbia were still the giants of the recorded music world in Britain but, towards the end of the decade, a new competitor moved in to battle for a slice of the action. Decca paraded a galaxy of stars poached from the big two – even Ambrose's big band defected to the new label – but there still seemed to be room in the market for everyone. Then, in America, the stock market crashed. And on both sides of the Atlantic, the spectre of mass unemployment brought down the curtain on the carefree years.

Marlene Dietrich in *The Blue Angel*. The later wartime song 'Lily Marlene' became a huge hit record.

Fred and Adele Astaire came to London in *Lady Be Good* and boosted dance records, while recording some themselves.

"AMOR PISZACY"

Marca da Fabrica depositada

Marca de Fábr

GRAMMOPHON
WORTMARKE.

"SCHREIBE

TRADE MARK

"GRAMOPHONE"

TRADE MARK
"GRAMMOPHON"

TRADE
GRAM

TRADE MARK
"GRAMMOPHON"

TRADE MARK
"GRAMMOPHON"

VÉD JEGY
"GRAMMOPHON"

TRADE MARK
(GRAMOPHONE.)

TRADE MARK
ПИШУЩ АМУРЪ

TRAD
GRAM

пишущий АМУРЪ
TRADE MARKE.

THE GREAT CLASSICS

In April 1922, Sir Edward Elgar opened The Gramophone Company's palatial new shop in Oxford Street, London. It was not so much the shop that caused a stir as the sign outside. Fifty feet long by thirty feet high, lit by 1,300 electric bulbs, it was one of London's first flickering 'action' signs: a man put a record on a gramophone, the turntable revolved and musical notes appeared from the speaker. Flashing bulbs, spreading like the rays of the sun, then pointed to the names of the Company's ten most illustrious artists, diplomatically arranged in alphabetical order: Caruso, Cortot, Elman, Galli-Curci, Gigli, Heifetz, Kreisler, Melba, Ruffo and Tetrazzini.

No popular singers, no music-hall artists, no jazz musicians were considered worthy of having their names in lights, for the classical repertoire was the Company's pride and joy, the backbone of its prestige, the envy of its competitors throughout the world. To be signed up as an HMV Red Label artist was considered an accolade in itself, instant recognition of international star status. And that fame was worth a fortune. Worldwide demand for classical records flourished after the First World War, and the prices of them varied in direct ratio to the prestige of the performer. Discs by a star violinist like Jascha Heifetz cost 8s 6d, whereas the same work by the obscure Alfredo Rode was worth only 4s 6d.

147

MILANO, VIA OREFICI, 2   May 17-1918

Dear Will:

Sabajno will be writing you about a new tenor named "Gigli" who has been singing in Rome and here and making an awful hit.

I have heard him and today I made a test of his voice. I tell you he is wonderful and don't hesitate to follow out Sabajno's advice about securing him because he is going to have a great career. You can discribe him as a 2nd Caruso except he has greater vocal flexibility. It is a real lyric voice that rings out all over the place o give you the impression of illimitable reserve 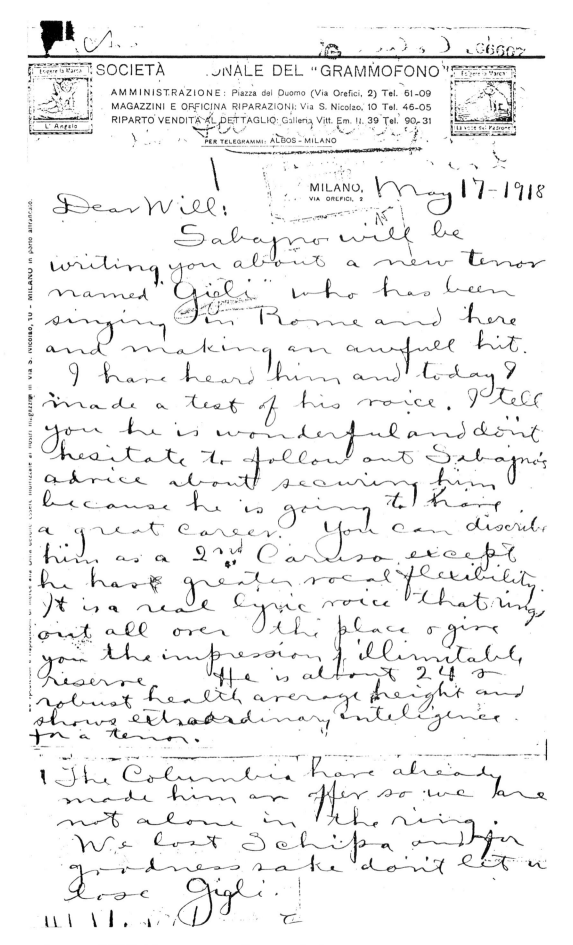 He is about 24 s robust health average height and shows extraordinary intelligence for a tenor.

The Columbia have already made him an offer so we are not alone in the ring. We lost Schipa and for goodness sake don't let us lose Gigli.

Letter to Will Gaisberg recommending a new Italian tenor, Beniamino Gigli (on right) as Cavaradossi in *Tosca*.

By 1923, top tenors were said to be earning around £30,000 a year from record royalties alone, with sopranos netting £17,000 and violinists £15,000.

HMV had concentrated its classical music efforts since 1910 on the talents of the great opera stars signed in the first decade of the century. When instrumental records were made, they tended to be by soloists or small groups of musicians. The acoustic recording system still posed problems with larger ensembles, producing sounds few concert-goers could enthuse over and few conductors were prepared to tolerate. Sir Edward Elgar was a rare exception. He was delighted and excited by a trial recording of *Carissima* which he made at City Road under Fred Gaisberg's expert guidance, and from 1914 was an influential support of the gramophone, recording frequently. His discs were accompanied by testimonials cajoling wary record buyers to listen. In 1917, an HMV release of Elgar conducting his own Violin Concerto had a note from him declaring that he was 'quite satisfied that the records of my composition are remarkably faithful reproductions of the originals'.

In the same year, the London String Quartet, under Alfred Hobday, had bravely completed a recording of Mozart's Clarinet Quintet in G Minor for Columbia during the first air-raid on London on 13 June 1917. They continued playing on the top floor of Columbia's offices in Clerkenwell Road, even when bombs were dropping less than half a mile away. The fact that those explosions could not be heard on the records later released said a lot about the limitations of the recording horn.

Felix Weingartner and his orchestra

Recognizing the futility of trying to compete with HMV's unbeatable array of soloists, Columbia decided to expand its recording of orchestras, despite the problems. In 1915, it signed young conductor Thomas Beecham, who had recorded first in 1910, and Sir Henry Wood, founder of the famous Promenade Concerts. Sir Henry was quite a catch, for previously he had refused to make records, saying the acoustic process could not reproduce strings satisfactorily. When Columbia released a disc of him conducting *Till Eulenspiegel's Merry Pranks*, Sir Henry's testimonial read: 'In my opinion, the greatest orchestral recording yet produced'.

The early Columbia orchestral releases were extremely popular. Indeed, sales were so encouraging that The Gramophone Company was forced to respond by stepping up its own recording programme, and the two companies began a race to produce bigger and better orchestral pieces. Some critics were outraged because works by Mozart, Tchaikovsky, Stravinsky and Strauss had to be mutilated to fit the eight-minute playing-time available on a double-sided twelve-inch disc. But in September 1923 the two companies came up with an idea which, though not entirely new, pleased both the critics and the public.

Columbia issued, on ten sides, a complete recording of Beethoven's Seventh Symphony, played by the London Symphony Orchestra under Felix Weingartner. HMV replied by releasing Tchaikovsky's *Pathétique*, almost complete, with the Royal Albert Hall Orchestra, conducted by the now-knighted Sir Landon Ronald. More complete classical masterpieces quickly followed: Dvořák's New World Symphony, Beethoven's Eighth and

Felix Weingartner, the Dalmatian conductor who exerted a great influence in shaping musical tastes in the performance of symphonic music in the present century. He held many important musical directorships during his life especially in Berlin and Vienna and made a substantial number of recordings between 1910 and 1940, almost all for the British Columbia company.

Milano 10 Ottobre 913

The Gramophone Company Ltd

Hayes. – Middlesex

The new records you have made of my voice have amazed me beyond words, so faithful and characteristic are they of my singing. The volume and general trueness are perfection itself, and I feel I would like to congratulate you on the complete success of the reproductions, which are artistic to the smallest detail.

Titta Ruffo

A letter of approval for the gramophone sound from the eminent singer Titta Ruffo.

Ninth, the Mozart Violin Concerto in A, Brahms' Second Symphony and the Tchaikovsky Fifth.

The two companies also competed fiercely for artists. After she made her London debut in 1924, HMV paraded the coloratura soprano Amelita Galli-Curci round its factories and shops like a prize trophy. It kept quiet about the fact that Galli-Curci, used to performing in large opera houses and concert-halls, found recording particularly difficult, and that her tendency to go above the note often meant as many as twenty-five attempts before a satisfactory master record was obtained.

Another of HMV's most successful artists, tenor Count John McCormack, had actually been handed to The Gramophone Company by Louis Sterling, boss of Columbia, when Sterling was still working for his phonograph company. McCormack had been discovered singing for pennies along the waterfront in Dublin and invited to make some cylinder recordings. Because in those days the cylinder and gramophone markets were thought to be separate, in late 1904 Sterling had allowed his exciting new tenor to record for his friend Fred Gaisberg at The Gramophone & Typewriter. Now he watched enviously as McCormack developed into one of the most popular recording artists in the world, earning upwards of £60,000 a year in royalties. In 1904, McCormack had received one guinea a title and, as a retaining fee, a gramophone and twenty-four records.

The constant quest for new talent made quick thinking and fast action essential. As a young man John Barbirolli recalled leaving the rostrum after conducting a concert as a

Titta Ruffo was an Italian operatic baritone blessed with both a magnificent voice and a strong natural acting ability. Famous for his performances of the great Verdi baritone roles such as Rigoletto and Iago, he also sang many other parts and left over 200 recorded examples of his distinctive interpretations.

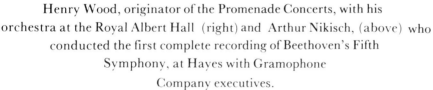

Henry Wood, originator of the Promenade Concerts, with his
orchestra at the Royal Albert Hall (right) and Arthur Nikisch, (above) who
conducted the first complete recording of Beethoven's Fifth
Symphony, at Hayes with Gramophone
Company executives.

last-minute replacement for Beecham who had been taken ill. 'When I was walking off the
platform after taking my bows,' he said, 'a man standing among the first fiddles attached
himself to me, and said, "My name's Gaisberg. Don't sign any contracts – I'll phone you in
the morning." '

The invention of the microphone and the arrival of electrical recording in 1925 at last
swept away the problem of having to range artists at varying distances around an acoustic
horn to achieve an acceptable balance. It also opened up the entire classical repertoire to
recording for the first time, allowing companies to capture even the largest operatic
ensembles on wax. Within a month of acquiring rights to the electrical process, HMV
began an-ambitious Wagner programme, with Albert Coates, universally acknowledged
England's finest conductor of Wagner, and later with Bruno Walter, the great German
conductor. For soloists, HMV had its pick of the best Wagnerian singers of the generation:
Friedrich Schorr, Florence Austral, Lotte Lehman, Frida Leider and the unforgettable

heroic tenor Lauritz Melchior. Florence Austral, one of HMV's most important sopranos throughout the '20s, also recorded the Church Scene from Gounod's *Faust* with Chaliapin. Fred Gaisberg, who arranged the session, recalled that it started in irreverent fashion: 'The singers crowded round in our small studio as the "SILENCE" signal buzzed, but Chaliapin could not resist the temptation to give the buxom Florence a sly pinch. So unexpected was it that she let out a squeal like a siren whistle.'

Another important advance made possible by microphones and the electric process was the recording of public performances. The first 'live' record, made at New York's Metropolitan Opera House in September 1925, featured 850 members of the Associated Glee Clubs of America, plus the audience of 4,000, singing '*Adeste Fideles*' and 'John Peel'. The disc, advertised as being by '4,850 singing voices', sounded loud and clear, with a resonance never before heard from a gramophone. Within a month of its release in Britain, the record was selling 2,000 copies a day.

John McCormack

HMV made its first attempt at recording a live performance when Dr Malcom Sargent conducted Handel's *Messiah* at the Royal Albert Hall. But the operation nearly ended in disaster. The new recording equipment was installed in a rented room behind the Alhambra Theatre in Leicester Square. Fred Gaisberg was in a box at the Albert Hall, ready to provide a running commentary over a telephone link-up so that the engineers would know when to start recording. At first everything went smoothly. As Dr Sargent walked on to the stage, Gaisberg whispered into his telephone: 'Any moment now, the conductor will be on the rostrum, start your machines . . .' The conductor tapped with his baton for silence and raised his arms. But at that moment, an anguished voice screeched over the telephone: 'Fred, for Gawd's sake, stop 'em!' The engineer had caught his telephone headset under the edge of the wax master record and lifted it off the machine. Gaisberg was hardly in a position to stand up in his box, in front of an audience of several thousand people, and ask the conductor to wait. Fortunately, a second machine was started just in time and the recording was saved.

Introducing microphones into the world's leading opera houses produced some bizarre moments, on stage and on record. Hidden in the footlights, the microphones were frequently too far away to pick up a solo voice at the back of the stage. This problem was explained to the tenor Giovanni Zenatello when HMV got permission to record *Otello* at Covent Garden. The singer decided to take matters into his own hands. Instead of delivering his entrance aria from the deck of the ship at the back of the stage, he clambered down from the poop, walked towards the audience, and stood directly over the microphone before bursting into the opening lines. The management were furious, claiming the production had been ruined and threatening to throw HMV and its recording equipment out of the opera house for ever. On another occasion, HMV was due to record an entire performance of *La Bohème*, also at Covent Garden. At the last moment one of the soloists stepped forward and demanded an extortionate fee. The Company, having spent months negotiating for permission to make the recording, paid up.

John McCormack, the famous Irish tenor, made a huge number of records, mostly for HMV, and his exceptional gifts of vocal purity and classical style were well suited to the requirements of recording. Although sometimes accused of not taking his music seriously enough, he achieved the highest standards of vocal art even in the lightest popular songs and ballads.

Early microphones had an unfortunate tendency to pick up extraneous sounds so a complete recording on fifty twelve-inch sides of *Tristan und Isolde*, with Kirsten Flagstad and Lauritz Mechior, was spoiled by stage noises, the whispering of the prompter and coughs and sneezes from the audience. Another ambitious HMV recording of a César Franck symphony in a cathedral was ruined when, at the end of the first movement, a lisping female voice was indelibly engaved in wax, saying: 'Tell me dear, where do you buy your stockings?' For years, that Franck work was referred to at HMV as the 'stockings symphony'. Another time, when a recording of *Gerontius* was being played back, shocked engineers heard a lady's voice talking about 'a lovely camisole for only eleven and sixpence'.

Most artists left the technical problems of recording to the engineers. Not so Leopold Stokowski, conductor of the Philadelphia Orchestra. In the studio he would endlessly shift microphones, adjust sound reflectors, rearrange the seating of the orchestra and involve himself in every detail. It was said that engineers at Victor, for whom Stokowski made many magnificent records, eventually fixed up a dummy set of control dials at his conducting podium, to keep him out of their way.

Towards the end of 1927, HMV produced – almost by chance – what was to become perhaps the most famous record ever made in Britain. The Company had fitted out a Lancia van as a mobile studio to cover concert performances and outdoor events such as the Aldershot Tattoo. One day, the mobile unit was at London's Temple Church making a whole series of recordings. At the end of the session, a couple of empty wax blanks were left over, so the engineers asked a choirboy, Ernest Lough, to fill them with two songs. They chose 'Hear My Prayer' and 'Oh, For The Wings Of A Dove'.

Vladimir de Pachmann, the Ukranian pianist is now best remembered for his eccentricities on the concert platform such as breaking off during a performance to address the audience. However, in spite of his sometimes odd behaviour, his recordings show him to have been an artist of exceptional talent, especially in the music of Chopin.

The child prodigy Yehudi Menuhin on the boat from New York to London. The year is 1927.

The record that resulted, C 1329, was issued without any kind of fanfare or publicity – indeed, one HMV manager queried the expense of the impromptu session – but it became one of the all-time best-sellers. Within weeks of its release, people were crowding into Temple Church at every service, standing on the pews to try to catch a glimpse of young Ernest filing in with the other choirboys. Critics praised the 'truly wonderful singing and reproduction' on the record, which carried on selling, year after year, for more than half a century.

Unfortunately for the record makers, not all artists were as easy to handle as Ernest Lough. The foibles and tantrums of some great names drove them to distraction. Studio manager Edward Fowler recalled the fuss when Russian pianist Vladimir de Pachmann arrived at HMV to make a record. Although it was the middle of June, the maestro arrived in a long, black, fur-lined overcoat. He sat down at the piano in the middle of the studio, played a few chords, then jumped to his feet and said: 'Impossible! The piano must be against the wall.' The piano was instantly moved. De Pachmann played a few more notes, but again leapt up. 'Impossible!' he said. 'I cannot play with all these lights. It must be dark.' Every light was turned off except the red recording monitor. The Russian made another attempt, played a little longer this time, then announced: 'Impossible to play without an audience. I must have an audience.' Twelve employees were marched to the studio from nearby offices. Again de Pachmann began to play, but after a couple of minutes he jumped up once again from the piano stool, ran across to the youngest man in the audience, threw his arms around his neck, and said: 'This I play for you, not The Gramophone Company.' The long-suffering engineers put up with such behaviour right through the session . . . but in the end their patience proved worthwhile – they got some fine records.

The bitter rivalry between Columbia and HMV continued to grow all through the '20s. In 1927, community singing enjoyed a brief popular revival. Columbia caught on first, and in January rushed out two discs of 2,500 voices singing 'Loch Lomond' and 'Shenandoah' at the Empire Theatre, Birmingham. HMV hit back immediately by recording 10,000 singers at the Royal Albert Hall. The following month, the two companies tried to outdo each other in celebrating Beethoven's centenary. Columbia produced twenty-nine major works on one hundred records, while HMV managed fourteen masterpieces on fifty-two discs.

The contest switched to Milan in 1928, when both rivals launched opera programmes, recording the works of Verdi, Puccini, Leoncavallo, Donizetti and Rossini. Lorenzo Molajoli conducted for Columbia, Carlo Sabajno for HMV. A success by one company provoked prompt retaliation from the other. When HMV released excellent recordings of the Beethoven and Brahms violin concertos by Fritz Kreisler, Columbia responded with versions of a similar quality by Joseph Szigeti.

The only real winners from such continual competition were gramophone owners. Never before had such a rich and varied choice of top-class classical records been available.

The violin concerto composed by Edward Elgar especially for the young Menuhin.

Elgar and Menuhin

But the golden days were to be cruelly cut short. Catastrophic events in America sent shock-waves across the Atlantic that were to change the whole shape of the record business in Britain.

Panic on Wall Street started on the morning of 24 October 1929. Rumour fed rumour on the floor of the New York Stock Exchange. For nearly two years there had been rash speculation in securities. Now, gripped by sudden fear, investors wanted their money out. After five days of frenetic selling, the market collapsed. The Great Depression had begun.

For the American recording industry, it was an unmitigated disaster. Sales plunged from 104 million records a year to less than six million. Within days of the Wall Street crash, Thomas Edison Incorporated announced that it would be making no more records or gramophones. Two big labels, Brunswick and Okeh, virtually stopped production. Columbia used its studio only for recording dance music. Victor, recently acquired by RCA, turned its factory at Camden, New Jersey, over to making wirelesses and began unloading its major artists.

Contracts being allowed to lapse were offered to HMV, RCA-Victor's British partner. Telegrams arrived at Hayes almost daily. A typical cable read: 'DROPPING DE LUCA AND HOROWITZ. ANY INTEREST? VICTOR.' Giuseppe de Luca was one of the finest baritones in the world and Vladimir Horowitz one of the most celebrated virtuoso pianists. HMV quickly snapped up both. Other artists made their own way to Europe. Violinist Jascha Heifetz telephoned Hayes one morning and asked Fred Gaisberg to meet him at the Berkeley Hotel. Over lunch, he confessed: 'Some people got out after the crash, some people were cleared out. I am one of the latter, I've got to get going again. What can you do to help me?' By the end of the meal, a contract had been drawn up.

The record business in Europe never slumped to quite the same extent as it did in America, but the harsh economic effects of the Depression did spread across the Atlantic. The combined profits of HMV and Columbia tumbled from £1,422,090 in 1930 to only £160,893 a year later. Secret top-level talks were already taking place between the two companies to discuss ways of halting the fall in profits and, on 20 March 1931, the arch rivals agreed that pooling resources was their only hope. They merged to form a new company, Electric and Musical Industries Limited, or E.M.I. HMV's Alfred Clark was appointed chairman, and Columbia's Louis Sterling became managing director of what was indisputably the biggest recording organization in the world. It owned fifty factories in nineteen different countries and, apart from *Deutsche Grammophon* in Germany, it had a virtual monopoly in Europe.

In fact, the biggest threat to E.M.I. came from within its own ranks. Despite the new image of friendly co-operation, the merger was not a happy one. Old and bitter rivalries could not be forgotten overnight, and staff from the two companies viewed each other with mutual loathing: Columbia employees considered HMV people snooty and old-fashioned;

Willem Mengelberg, on arrival in London, is met at the docks by Sir Thomas Beecham.

Arturo Toscanini arriving at the docks with his wife and daughter Wanda, later to marry
Vladimir Horowitz.

JASCHA
HEIFETZ

RECORDS EXCLUSIVELY FOR
"HIS MASTER'S VOICE"

L BARTON

Jascha Heifetz at home with his sister Pauline on piano

Benno Moiseiwitsch, the Russian pianist, accompanying his wife Daisy Kennedy Fraser

Bruno Walter at the Musikverein in Vienna, shortly before his last recording there, Mahler's Ninth Symphony, in 1938. Nazi stormtroopers arrived in the city before the record could be distributed.

HMV staff dismissed their new colleagues as unworthy, gimcrack upstarts. They had not forgotten the furore of 1927 when Columbia offered a £2,000 prize for the best completion of Schubert's Unfinished Symphony. Academics and HMV had been aghast at the idea. Now one HMV director snorted: 'Columbia people always arrive late for meetings, and almost always drunk.'

It was perhaps unfortunate for Columbia's reputation as a serious recording company that, on the very day the merger was announced, its engineers were at a seance trying to record the voice of a 'spirit' speaking through the well-known medium Meurig Morris. One of the observers, who had been strenuously opposed to the experiment, tried to ruin the recording by coughing loudly halfway through, while Mrs Morris was in a trance. She promised afterwards that the coughing would not be heard on the record – and she was right. But the sermon, delivered by the 'spirit' in a deep bass voice, excited little interest among record buyers.

The infant E.M.I. was hampered by another problem, even more disastrous than personal animosity. Its artists were allowed to carry on their exclusive label contracts. Thus if an HMV singer was appearing with a Columbia artist at Covent Garden, neither label could record the performance. Columbia records were not even stored in the E.M.I. archives for several years after the merger. Alfred Clark did not think they were worth keeping.

Not long before the HMV–Columbia marriage of convenience, workmen had moved into the leafy back garden of a large Regency villa in Abbey Road, St John's Wood, London, to build a huge orchestral recording studio. The villa itself was converted into smaller studios and offices and, by November 1931, what was said to be the largest building in the world devoted exclusively to recording was completed. As an opening ceremony, the London Symphony Orchestra recorded Sir Edward Elgar's *Falstaff* suite, conducted by the composer. With a cheery greeting to the musicians of 'Good morning, gentlemen, very light programme this morning! Please play this as if you have never heard it before', Sir Edward launched the studio on its long and illustrious career. During the following decades the finest singers and musicians in the world were to pass through its unprepossessing doors.

Artur Schnabel completed all thirty-two Beethoven piano sonatas and five concertos at Abbey Road during the '30s, but none of the sessions was easy: on his first visit, Schnabel slowly paced the floor with all eyes anxiously watching him, then stopped in the middle of the studio and announced: 'I play *here*.' The carefully positioned piano was hastily wheeled to the spot where the maestro was standing, and he began his epic recording marathon. At a later session, an engineer asked Schnabel to modify a passage for the recording, and the pianist flew into a terrible rage. 'Beethoven wanted it *so*!' he shouted, and played the passage. 'I teach my pupils *so*!' he ranted, repeating the performance. 'When I play in the concert hall, I play it *so*! Now when your recording apparatus can make it *so*, we start again.' Another time, twenty-nine waxes were wasted on the making of a single record because

Jacques Thibaud

Pablo Casals   Alfred Cortot

Schnabel kept stopping. He would bang down the lid of the piano, kick the stool away and pace the studio floor muttering, 'Impossible! Impossible!' It took nearly a decade to complete the fifteen volumes of more than one hundred records.

Such ambitious and expensive programmes were made possible by an ingenious marketing idea dreamed up by a young employee, Walter Legge. He suggested forming societies devoted to different composers, and inviting record buyers to subscribe in advance for their works. Recording would begin only when the number of subscribers made it economically feasible. It was a brilliantly successful concept, and enabled classical recording to continue right through the Depression years. Legge, who had been employed originally as editor of the Company house magazine, *The Voice*, switched to the Artists' Department and eventually became one of the country's most influential classical record producers.

The first of the societies was devoted to the beautiful but difficult songs of Hugo Wolf. In October 1931, HMV advertised for subscribers willing to pay thirty shillings (£1.50) for an album of six records to be sung by Elena Gerhardt. By December, the Hugo Wolf Society was fully subscribed with five hundred members, and the first volume, now much prized by collectors, was issued in April 1932. Other societies soon followed, greatly extending E.M.I.'s classical repertoire. Sir Thomas Beecham, Sir Adrian Boult and others conducted the Sibelius symphonies and tone poems. Albert Schweitzer, who used recording fees to finance his mission hospital in Africa, performed Bach's organ music. Fritz Kreisler and Franz Rupp played Beethoven's ten violin sonatas, the Pro Arte String Quartet completed all twenty-nine Haydn quartets, and Wanda Landowska's harpsichord interpretations of music by Bach, Handel and Scarlatti led to a revival of interest in the instrument throughout Europe.

Alfred Cortot, Jacques Thibaud and Pablo Casals were three of the most distinguished soloists of this century who also regularly played together as a trio. Of the many superb recordings they made together for HMV, the Beethoven Archduke Trio is undoubtedly the best known.

George Bernard Shaw was one of many illustrious authors, actors and statesmen who recorded the spoken word.

Albert Schweitzer, who used his recording fees from organ concerts to finance his leper colony and hospital in the African jungle.

Each artist had a unique approach to recording. Violinist Fritz Kreisler, for example, played in his carpet-slippers to stop inadvertent squeaks from his outdoor shoes marring the records. He always arrived early in the studio with a humidity meter, which he used to decide whether to play his Stradivarius or his Guarnerius. While he was playing one, the other would be left carelessly lying about. He explained: 'My violins are so well-known, it doesn't matter how casual I am about them, I don't see how they could fail to come back.'

For years, HMV had tried to book Kreisler to play Elgar's Violin Concerto with the composer conducting, but a mutually acceptable date could never be agreed. In 1932, with Sir Edward seventy-five years old and in failing health, the company decided to find an alternative soloist. It chose a fifteen-year-old boy prodigy, Yehudi Menuhin. The youngster and the grand old man of music got along famously, and the record they made together at Abbey Road, in July 1932, is one of the milestones of recorded music. Two weeks after the session, Menuhin and Elgar repeated their triumphant performance in concert at the Albert Hall and the Pleyel Hall in Paris. For Menuhin, it was the beginning of a brilliant fifty-year career as an HMV recording artist. For Elgar, it was almost the final chapter of an illustrious lifetime. In January 1934 – twenty years after his first recording – he was seriously ill in bed when the London Symphony Orchestra under Lawrence Collingwood recorded his *Caractacus*. E.M.I. organized a telephone link-up from the studio to the great

◄Wanda Landowska, who re-established the harpsichord as a serious instrument with her superb renditions of Bach, Handel and Scarlatti

Artur Rubinstein

Artur Schnabel

Vladimir Horowitz

Artur Schnabel, the Austrian pianist whose recordings of the complete Beethoven Piano Sonatas made throughout the nineteen thirties remain unsurpassed to this day as a unique artistic achievement.

Artur Rubinstein and Vladimir Horowitz, considered to be the finest pianists of their time, were also the most widely heard artists through their records. Born in Poland and Russia respectively, both made recordings for HMV in London at the start of their international careers. Both subsequently settled in the USA and have each continued to record (for RCA and CBS) for over half a century.

◄Sergei Rachmaninov's recording career was as composer and performer. In 1918 he started a twenty-year cycle as a supreme international pianist, recording and performing Bach and the romantics, as well as his own compositions.

Maria Jeritza, the glamorous and talented Czech soprano and tenor Richard Tauber, (right) who became one of the heart-throbs of his time as the leading singer in most of Franz Léhar's operettas.

Elisabeth Schumann, soprano, the foremost lieder singer of her time.

man's bedside so that he could hear and comment on the performance. He was delighted to do so, and contributed some helpful ideas. On 23 February, Elgar died, and the gramophone lost one of its most valuable friends, a man whose contribution to establishing E.M.I.'s pre-eminence in classical music had been priceless.

By the mid '30s, E.M.I. had attracted almost all the finest classical artists in the world. No recording company had ever had such a concentration of talent under contract. Only three famous names were absent from the catalogue – Italian maestro Arturo Toscanini who hated recording, the German conductor Wilhelm Furtwängler, and Lotte Lehman, both under contract to *Deutsche Grammophon* – but before the decade was out, all three had joined E.M.I.

Toscanini had tried recording in 1929, but the constant stopping and starting as wax blanks were changed irritated him to such an extent that, at the end of the session, he muttered: 'Never again!' In 1931, RCA–Victor secretly recorded him conducting Beethoven's Fifth at New York's Carnegie Hall, to try to persuade him to change his mind. But he was so appalled when he listened to the test pressings that he insisted on the master records being destroyed. It was 1935 before he could be persuaded to try again, this time in London. After persistent pressure from E.M.I., Toscanini grudgingly agreed to record a Brahms concert with the BBC Symphony Orchestra at Queen's Hall, on condition that the recording process did not interfere in any way with the performance. There were to be no buzzers or warning lights, no visible engineers or machinery, and no question of stopping the performance once it had started. Despite heroic efforts by the engineers, the recording was not an unqualified success.

Lauritz Melchior, the Danish baritone who later became a powerful tenor and major interpreter ►
of Richard Wagner's music, is seen here as Lohengrin.

Elsa Stralia
Australian dramatic soprano

Amelita Galli-Curci
Italian coloratura soprano

Frieda Hempel   Rosa Ponselle
German coloratura soprano   American dramatic soprano

SUPPLÉMENT

GOR STRAWINSSKI

ENREGISTREMENTS ÉLECTRIQUE

LA VOIX DE SON MAITRE

La Voix de son Maître

COMPAGNIE FRANÇAISE DU GRAMOPHONE

Later, Toscanini surprised everyone by agreeing to conduct the same orchestra at the Abbey Road studio. It was one of the shortest recording sessions ever. The maestro arrived in a bad temper, and his mood grew even blacker when he was escorted into the studio and saw that the orchestra was not laid out in the way it had been at the Queen's Hall. For a few minutes he refused to take the rostrum, merely glaring at the players, who shifted uncomfortably in their seats. Finally, he took his place, gave two taps on the music stand and raised his baton. The orchestra played twenty bars, then Toscanini stopped them, announced he did not like the placing of the instruments, and swept out of the room. His car was disappearing down Abbey Road before anyone realized what had happened. A lot more patient coaxing was necessary before Toscanini was at last wooed into the E.M.I. fold.

Luckily, most other conductors were easier to work with. Sir Thomas Beecham made many inspired records with the orchestra he helped to found, the London Philharmonic. Felix Weingartner, Clemens Kraus, Bruno Walter and Erich Kleiber all brought the best out of the Vienna Philharmonic, Furtwängler recorded with the Berlin Philharmonic, and Sir Adrian Boult conducted the BBC Symphony Orchestra.

Hand in hand with the orchestral programme, HMV was maintaining its reputation as the leading company for opera. When the Glyndebourne Festival was founded in 1934, it signed an exclusive contract to record each season. The complete operas of *Figaro, Cosi Fan Tutte* and *Don Giovanni* were among the first discs to be released. And at La Scala, Milan, the tenor Beniamino Gigli recorded *Pagliacci* and *La Bohème* with great success. Gigli was a much-loved HMV artist, always keen to make records and earn *lire*. Once, he prevented an expensive project to record *Tosca* in Rome from ending in disaster. The leading soprano, Iva Paceti, collapsed, and a doctor called to the opera house prescribed three days' complete rest – exactly the time left to finish the session. As the orchestra and chorus of 150 waited, Gigli telephoned his friend, Maria Caniglia, to ask if she would like to sing *Tosca* with him. 'I am still half asleep,' she said, 'and I haven't sung the role for months. When do you want me to do it?' Gigli replied, 'Now.' Within an hour, the new soprano was at the opera house, singing the love duet from the first act.

As the threat of war loomed once more over Europe, E.M.I. teams hurried from country to country, filling gaps in the classical catalogue. In Prague, Pablo Casals recorded Dvořák's Cello Concerto with the Czech Philharmonic Orchestra. At Vienna's old Musikverein, Bruno Walter conducted Mahler's Ninth Symphony with the Vienna Philharmonic. Nazi stormtroopers were in the Austrian capital before the records could be issued. Weingartner was recorded in Paris, and at Lucerne the troublesome Toscanini was captured on disc at the Summer Festival. A month later, war was declared.

In London, shortly before the outbreak of war, Artur Rubinstein completed the remarkable feat of recording all fifty-two Chopin mazurkas in less than four weeks at Abbey Road. But Hitler ended such ambitious sessions. Air-raids made it more and more difficult to assemble the musicians, and many of the great artists left for America. Supplies of shellac became scarce, and most of the Hayes factory was again given over to making munitions.

◄Igor Stravinsky catalogue, HMV France. Starting as a student of Rimsky-Korsakov in 1929, he became arguably the greatest composer of the twentieth century and composing's *enfant terrible*.

Carded

JACK HYLTON

NUOVI DISCHI DANZE

INCISIONE ELETTRICA

S.A. NAZIONALE DEL GRAMMOFONO

THE RISE & FALL
OF THE BIG BANDS

The grim economic realities of life after the crash of 1929 affected everyone in America. Several record companies went bust, including the pioneering Gennett organization, which had recorded many of the early Midwest jazz bands. Those companies that stayed in business had to restrict themselves to certainties, the commercial numbers that were sure to sell. And in the anxious early '30s, 'commercial' meant smooth and sentimental big-band sounds that made few demands on the ears of listeners, and dreamy, romantic ballads that, as one critic wrote, 'soothed the white man's pain as the blues had salved the black man's troubles'. The hit songs now were 'I Can't Give You Anything But Love Baby', 'How Deep Is The Ocean' and 'Buddy, Can You Spare A Dime'.

The bands that rode the storm were those that risked the scorn of professional critics and compromised to tune in to the public's hunger for escapism. Orchestras grew more disciplined, playing to tighter arrangements. Solos that had been raucous became refined, now ornamental instead of exciting and improvisational. They provided 'melodies that you can hang your hat on'.

Paul Whiteman was still going strong. In the '20s he had taken dance music out of the cornet-sax-fiddle-banjo-sousaphone stage by encouraging arrangers, featuring star singers and adopting techniques from the classical orchestras in which he had served his apprenticeship. Now more bandleaders followed his example. Gus Arnheim, who had been part of the hot-jazz scene in Chicago, took up residence at the Coconut Grove in Los Angeles, and hired Whiteman's singing group, the Rhythm Boys. His nightly two-hour radio broadcasts helped to launch Bing Crosby to international stardom, and popularized such hits as 'Wrap Your Troubles In Dreams' and 'I Surrender, Dear'.

Guy Lombardo and his Royal Canadians had built their reputation for 'the sweetest music this side of Heaven' in Cleveland and Chicago. In 1929 they appeared for the first

time in New York, at the Hotel Roosevelt Grill Room. Lombardo was to return for a season there every year except one until 1962. 'We rode in on Paul Whiteman's coat-tails,' he said. Though many jazz fans detested the saccharine sounds, Lombardo, whose rhythm section was felt rather than heard, reaped a rich harvest from giving the public what they wanted. He recorded first with Columbia, then with the infant Decca company, and sold more than 25 million records over forty years. Louis Armstrong stunned some of his own followers by admitting that he was one of Lombardo's greatest admirers, and the band also achieved the distinction of drawing the largest-ever crowd to a former hotbed of jazz, Harlem's Savoy Ballroom. 'By 1934,' Lombardo said, 'if you didn't play like us, you couldn't get a job.'

Other leaders were quick to learn that lesson. Hal Kemp produced such sweet best-sellers as 'Got A Date With An Angel' and 'The Touch Of Your Lips', and Leo Reisman, who recorded RCA–Victor's first experimental LP record in 1931, cashed in on melodic show-tunes such as 'Time On My Hands', 'Stormy Weather' and 'Night And Day'. His vocalists included Fred Astaire and Dinah Shore. Ted Weems was another steady seller for Victor, although 'Heartaches', which he recorded in 1933, did not become a million-seller until after an unexpected radio airplay in 1947.

The players in such bands were true professionals – and they had to be. Recording-studio time was precious, and often the musicians were seeing the music for the first time when they arrived for the session. Good musicianship, speed and accuracy were essential when four, sometimes six, numbers had to be completed in three hours. A new song had to be rush-released to stop a rival band establishing it as a hit, and it had to be recorded at one take on to the wax or acetate master disc. It would be 1948 before tape started to make its appearance, enabling parts of different performances to be spliced together. And there were no electronic gimmicks to disguise shortcomings, though sounds did improve after Columbia engineer Morty Palitz devised the first echo chamber – putting microphones and players in the men's room!

Louis Armstrong was leading a big band of his own by 1934, recording scores of currently popular songs for various companies. Like most jazz musicians who carried on, Louis had to restrain his natural inclination and tone down his music to suit the mood of the '30s. It would be some years before Duke Ellington's immortal line, 'It don't mean a thing if it ain't got that swing', proved true. Many who despaired of the direction music had taken in America now found that the most exciting sounds came, not from their own land, but from Britain. And their surprise was matched only by that of the record company who suddenly found themselves with one of the hottest properties in the world.

Although Britain too was hit by the Depression, you would hardly have guessed it most nights in London's West End. The privileged classes still demanded a glittering nightlife, and there were plenty of classy bands around to provide it. Apart from the no-expenses-spared revels at the Savoy, Jack Payne's band was at the Cecil Hotel, Ben Davis kept the

◄Gracie Fields, England's pre-eminent musical comedienne, recorded many major film musicals of the '30s and '40s.

Carlton dancing, Harry Roy delighted the Café Anglais, American Al Starita called the tune at the Piccadilly, Jack Jackson was jumping at the Dorchester, and Bert Ambrose still reigned supreme at the Mayfair. The big record companies had all the top bands under contract, but they also had their own studio orchestras, often composed of sidemen from the star bands, who helped to provide disc dance music for those who could not join the West End whirl.

HMV's house band, known as the New Mayfair Orchestra, had been formed in 1928, under the baton of the company's light music director, Carroll Gibbons, who was also leader of the elite Savoy Orpheans. When, in July 1929, he was offered a Hollywood contract by the MGM group, he recommended as his replacement a promising twenty-two-year-old arranger then working for the BBC – Ray Noble.

When Noble arrived at HMV to take over the house band, Jack Hylton and Bert Ambrose were still the label top-liners, followed by Jack Payne and the man who was to succeed him as the leader of the BBC Dance Orchestra, Henry Hall. Last in line, Noble had to make out as best he could with the tunes they did not want. Yet within three years his imaginative arrangements, perfectionist attention to detail and control of the players he selected – top sidesmen from the Ambrose, Savoy and Roy Fox orchestras – were to make him a bigger seller than all the big names. He had two further advantages over his label rivals: a singer called Al Bowlly and an ability to write hit songs such as 'Goodnight Sweetheart' (1931), 'Love Is The Sweetest Thing' (1932) and 'The Very Thought Of You' (1934). His records amazed HMV. Not only did they sell well in Britain, but they were a staggering success in America when Victor issued them there. As his popularity grew, the name on the discs changed from the anonymous New Mayfair Orchestra to Ray Noble and the New Mayfair Orchestra, and finally the Ray Noble Orchestra. And when both Hylton and Ambrose defected to the new Decca company, Noble's steady stream of hits cushioned the blow.

With Al Bowlly, Noble had found the voice that matched his music perfectly. Bowlly, born in Lourenço Marques, Mozambique, in 1890, arrived in Britain in July 1928 after adventures with jazz bands in Africa, India – where he recorded at HMV's Dum Dum studio – and Germany. He already had a reputation as a ladykiller, as American Don Barrigo, who played tenor sax behind him in Berlin, confirmed: 'That Bowlly could bring the weeps on any dame at any time, just by looking at them with his dark eyes and working his tonsils.' But success as a singer then did not bring the riches it does today. Vocalists were still considered members of the band, called forward for thirty-two bars, then sent back to the ranks. When one orchestra folded, after a disastrous Scottish tour, on Christmas Eve

Bert Ambrose and his Embassy Club Orchestra (left) Ray Noble and his band (above).

1929, Bowlly was so hard up he spent a week busking on London streets . . . and picked up £2 17s. Bowlly and Ray Noble made their first record together in November 1930, and by 1932 had combined on more than two hundred tracks. From 1929 until his death in 1941, Bowlly was to record for twenty-seven different labels. In one typical two-month spell, October – November 1930, he cut forty-eight masters in fourteen sessions.

In 1931 Bowlly was hired by Roy Fox, the 'whispering cornetist', for the opening of the Monseigneur Club, a plush new nightspot on the corner of Piccadilly and Lower Regent Street. It quickly became the in-place with smart society, patronized by the then Prince of Wales – later to abdicate as King Edward – and the Maharanee of Sarawak. And when the BBC began live broadcasts, Bowlly and Fox soon became idols. Bowlly's dark good looks and sparkling smile – he attributed his gleaming white teeth to his habit of eating chicken bones – drew the eye of every lady in the club, and millions listening at home fell in love with his intimate crooning.

Meanwhile, the astonishing success of Ray Noble's records increased pressure on HMV to let their star orchestra be seen in concert. The problem was that it existed only on record. When Ray Noble did at last make a public appearance, it was with Lew Stone's band, which he had 'borrowed' for a month-long series of concerts at the top Dutch beach resort of Scheveningen.

In the summer of 1934, Noble was invited to perform in America – a rare reversal of the normal west-to-east traffic in star musicians. Union problems prevented him taking British players with him, but he insisted on taking Al Bowlly along. A former Ben Pollack protégé called Glenn Miller put together a star-studded line-up for Noble and they opened in the exclusive Rainbow Room, on the sixty-fifth floor of the RCA building in Radio City, in 1935, receiving an enthusiastic welcome. Critic George Simon wrote: 'Everything points to this becoming one of the great all-round bands of all time. Noble, suave and sophisticated, arranges ballads with great musical taste and tenderness. And with the jazz-wise Miller to take care of that department, the band appears to have all bases covered.'

Noble's new orchestra recorded on the Victor label, producing such hits as 'Soon', 'Down By The River', 'My Melancholy Baby', 'I Wished On The Moon', and a Noble song, 'Why Stars Come Out At Night'. The discs and regular radio work brought vocalist Bowlly massive fan-mail. One of his favourite letters said: 'When your voice comes on the air, it's just like fizzy lemonade being poured down my spine.' In 1936, Noble took the band on a tour of one-night stands, college dances and movie theatres. They were doing five shows a day at some venues, seven a day at the Paramount in New York. That same year, readers of *Metronome* magazine voted Bowlly second-best vocalist in America, one place ahead of Bing Crosby. The Casa Loma's Kenny Sargent came first.

◄George Formby Jr, the ukulele man, carried on the tradition of his father, (left) the great music-hall artist at the turn of the century.

But the glory days for Bowlly were almost at an end. When Ray Noble accepted an offer to work on the successful Burns and Allen radio show in Los Angeles, Bowlly elected to return to England, and sailed from New York in January 1937. Little did he know that he was turning his back on his best chance of finding even greater fame and fortune, and returning to a city that was no longer the centre of attention. For the pendulum of popular music was swinging back to America – and swing was the operative word.

Benny Goodman had had a terrible three months. He had lost radio exposure on fifty-three stations when the National Biscuit Company axed *Let's Dance*, the show it sponsored to promote its latest line, Ritz crackers. Then the Goodman band was given notice to quit on the first night of an engagement at New York's plush Roosevelt Hotel, home of super-sweet Guy Lombardo. 'Every time I looked around, one of the waiters or the captain would be motioning us not to play so loud,' said Goodman.

Now a road tour of the Midwest was flopping. Audiences at Toledo, Lakeside in Michigan, Milwaukee and Denver had been apathetic. At Elitch's Gardens on the edge of the Rockies came what Goodman was to call 'just about the most humiliating moment of my life'. The manager complained that customers were demanding their money back, and insisted on waltzes for the rest of the band's four-week stay. As his players piled into four cars for the long drive to the next gig in California, Goodman, twenty-six, a former clarinettist with Ben Pollack's big band, was seriously thinking of disbanding his one-year-old outfit and returning to the New York recording studios where he had earned a living as a session man since 1928.

But that next gig was to change everything – both for Goodman and for popular music. The band was wary as it took the stand at the Palomar Ballroom, Los Angeles, on 21 August 1935. 'We played the first couple of sets under wraps,' recalled drummer Gene Krupa. 'We weren't getting much reaction, so Benny decided, to hell with playing safe, and we started playing hot numbers. Well, from then on we were in.' Goodman himself said: 'Before we'd played four bars of "King Porter Stomp", there was such yelling and stomping and carrying on in that hall, I thought a riot had broken out . . .' In a way it had. A riot that was to last for the next six years.

America could see light at the end of the Depression tunnel. The election of President Franklin D. Roosevelt had unleashed a wave of optimism that was as contagious as spring fever. His New Deal offered hope of a brighter future. Suddenly young Americans were ready to dance again, kicking aside the syrup-sweet music of sentimental self-pity, hungry for excitement.

Goodman had sensed the mood. He had hired jazz-minded bandleader Fletcher Henderson to re-create the scores that had set New York's Roseland Ballroom rocking in the '20s. Top jazz sidesmen such as Krupa and trumpeter Bunny Berrigan were part of a line-up designed to put new life into a dead music-scene. But for twelve months it seemed that

The stage musical provided endless talent for recording companies. Cicely Courtneidge, Stanley Holloway, Tessie O'Shea and Jack Buchanan epitomized the genre of music and revue at the time. ▶

Tessie O'Shea

Jack Buchanan

Cicely Courtneidge

Stanley Holloway

Sasha Guitry, the French star actor who counted Yvonne Printemps, a singer of the period,
among his several wives. They recorded some sessions together.

America was not ready for the change; promotors insisted that the band stick to safe, standard numbers. Now, as Goodman savoured the sound of the kids who clustered round the Palomar bandstand, a new era was dawning . . . the golden age of swing.

The journey back east was a complete contrast to the band's sad trek west. In Goodman's hometown of Chicago, they were booked for three weeks at the Congress Hotel. It was eight months before an adoring public would allow the newly nicknamed King of Swing to leave. When he opened at the Paramount Theatre in New York, queues began to form at 7 a.m. Bobbysoxers leapt from their seats to dance a frenzied jitterbug in the aisles. Police ringed the stage to protect the players from over-enthusiastic adulation. Firemen were called in to cool dance riots with their hoses.

Goodman was to set new standards for popular music, extending its scope and respectability, establishing new rules. In the process he was to make himself a millionaire. He produced a succession of massive hits – 'Sometimes I'm Happy', 'One O'Clock Jump', 'Sing Sing Sing', 'You Turned The Tables On Me' – first for Victor, then, from 1939, for Columbia. His band and the small all-star groups he formed within it played venues previously considered the exclusive preserve of classical musicians. And he forced a new kind of response from audiences. Big bands were no longer just for listening to and dancing to – they were for watching and worshipping.

Another of Goodman's achievements was in breaking through the race barrier that still bedevilled American popular music. Encouraged by jazz buff John Hammond, later a Columbia Records executive, Goodman tried out a young black pianist called Teddy Wilson on his Goodman Trio records. Then, without fanfare, he put him on stage with the full band at concerts. When Leo Reisman had tried letting black and white musicians play together in public in 1929, some of the New York audience had walked out. Nobody walked out on Goodman. Soon more black stars joined the band: inspirational, perspirational Lionel Hampton in the rhythm section, Charlie Christian on the electric guitar he had invented. The best in the business worked for Benny Goodman, regardless of the colour of their skin.

Noël Coward became both a recording star and a major songwriter and producer on both sides of the Atlantic. Gertrude (Gertie) Lawrence and Beatrice (Bea) Lillie were often his partners on records and on stage.

The popular comedy team, Flanagan and Allen, which supplied the songs to match the spirit of British troops in the Second World War.

Joe Loss's dance orchestra – a major recording staple for fifty years.

Swing, like jazz before it, was attacked by reactionaries. A *New York Times* article claimed it could be responsible for emotional imbalance and sexual excesses such as rape because it was 'cunningly devised to a faster tempo than 72 bars to the minute – faster than the human pulse'. It certainly set human pulses racing. Other bands were quick to follow Goodman's lead and raise the tempo. And by the late '30s New York could offer dance fans possibly the greatest galaxy of talent ever assembled in one city.

Goodman's band had taken up residence at the Madhatten room of the Hotel Pennsylvania, Jimmy Dorsey's men were at the Hotel New Yorker, Artie Shaw was entertaining at the Hotel Lincoln, Les Brown, later to discover the singer Doris Day, was at the Hotel Edison, and Bob Crosby, Bing's brother, was offering 'the happiest music in the world' with his Dixieland Bob Cats at the Lexington. Jazz giants Jimmie Lunceford and Chick Webb were still in town, and Count Basie, 'rediscovered' by John Hammond in Kansas, performed at the Famous Door Club. Duke Ellington continued to finance his sophisticated symphonic ambitions by recording hit songs such as 'Mood Indigo', 'Satin Doll' and 'Take The A Train'. When asked by critic George Simon how he felt about white bands grabbing the glory for music similar to that which he had been playing for years, the suave Duke replied: 'Competition only makes you play better. Besides, a guy may go to a lot of fancy restaurants, but he always comes home to that soul food.'

Bing Crosby, the first crooner, started with the Paul Whiteman Band and became the most successful solo recording artist of his time. Here, in a film with Marjorie Reynolds.

Harry James, with Glenn Miller the last of the great Swing bands, gave Frank Sinatra his start only to lose him to Tommy Dorsey. He then cut down on Swing, added strings and the rich voice of Dick Haymes, to become an all-time record money-spinner. His wartime songs especially were smash hits.

Also in New York at that time was the second of the swing superbands, the Tommy Dorsey Orchestra. Tommy and his brother Jimmy had learned the basics in the Paul Whiteman band. In the mid '30s they formed an eleven-piece band of their own which included trombonist Glenn Miller. But when Miller left to form the Ray Noble band, the Dorseys, temperamentally very different, split up. The inevitable break came during a concert at the Glen Island Casino. Tommy, a volatile, forceful, driving character, beat off the tempo for a song called 'I'll Never Say Never Again Again'. Jimmy, more easy-going, said he thought the beat was a little too fast. His brother picked up his horn and stormed off the stand.

Tommy took over the band of Joe Haymes, which was playing New York's McAlpin Hotel, but failing to set the world alight. Using the arranging talents of Paul Weston and Sy Oliver, hiring jazz big names such as drummer Davey Tough and Bunny Berrigan, and finding a vocalist called Jack Leonard, who for several years rivalled Crosby as the kids' favourite singer, Dorsey quickly made a name for himself as the Sentimental Gentleman of Swing.

He recorded a string of hits for Victor – 'For Sentimental Reasons', 'Dedicated To You', 'Little White Lies', 'You Taught Me To Live Again', 'Once In A While', and 'Marie'. Dorsey first heard 'Marie' in Philadelphia, played by a coloured band who were sharing the bill, the Royal Sunset Serenaders. 'I figured we could do more with it than they could,' he said. 'So I traded them eight of our arrangements for that one of theirs.'

When Jack Leonard left in 1940, Dorsey had problems finding a replacement. He was advised to check on 'that skinny kid with James' – Frank Sinatra. Harry James's band was

Benny Goodman, the father of Swing, projected the clarinet into the Swing sound. If you didn't play like Goodman and his band, you couldn't get a job.

Count Basie Band, here with Ethel Waters as soloist, recorded first for Columbia and then for the Victor Company.

not doing very well by the time it reached Chicago's Sherman Hotel in 1940. Dorsey, at the nearby Palmer House, was a much better prospect for the singer from Hoboken, especially as his wife Nancy was expecting a child. James agreed to waive the last five months of his contract, and signed Dick Haymes as replacement. Dorsey, delighted with his capture, predicted that his new singer would become as big as Bing Crosby.

Sinatra, who said that being a big-band vocalist was 'the end of the rainbow for any singer who wanted to make it', never forgot Dorsey's influence on him. Before he left the band for even greater things in 1942 – to be followed again by Dick Haymes – Dorsey's gentle, rocking, rhythmic swing had earned him enormous recording hits with 'Easy Does It', 'Chicago' and 'The Sunny Side Of The Street'.

Dorsey, like Goodman, earned more than a million dollars from his music over the years. In the '50s he got together again with brother Jimmy to work on a TV series, and the two men died within six months of each other in 1957. By then the golden age of the big bands was just a nostalgic memory. The seeds of their decline were being sown even while Tommy was at his peak.

In 1942, the American Federation of Musicians, led by James C. Petrillo, demanded huge compensation payments from the big three record companies, RCA–Victor, Columbia and Decca, claiming the use of discs on the growing number of jukeboxes and radio stations was restricting live music and throwing his musicians out of work. When the companies refused to pay up, Petrillo ignored the pleas of the bandsmen and called an all-out strike which was to last for more than a year. Decca capitulated first, in September 1943. Victor and Columbia held out until November 1944. Petrillo claimed he had won 'the greatest victory in the history of the labour movement', but it was no victory for the big bands. While they had been barred from recording studios, their vocalists had been recording without instrumental backing and scoring some impressive hits. The singers had almost replaced their employers as No. 1 public idols. And because the strike did not affect smaller record companies, who put the emphasis on blues and country music, those styles again increased their foothold in the music market.

The war had also hit many bands: a lot of the top players were drafted; petrol shortages restricted travel both for bands and for their audiences. Out-of-town venues were forced to close. A midnight curfew 'brownout' was imposed, and a twenty-per-cent entertainment tax persuaded many restaurants, hotels and clubs to stop serving music with their meals. In addition, the mood of America was subtly shifting: sentiment was once more back in fashion as young men left their wives and sweethearts to go to war, or snatched romance on all-too-short spells of leave. The last two superbands of the swing era had leaders who recognized that times were changing. They were Glenn Miller and Harry James.

Glenn Miller struggled for the first two years after deciding to set up a band of his own in 1937, but on 1 March 1939, his thirty-fifth birthday, he got the break he had been waiting for when the Glen Island Casino in New York booked him for the summer. With the date

went a regular radio spot, and Miller's distinctive, gently swinging style quickly earned him a large following. When the band went on tour in the autumn, they smashed attendance records at a string of venues. And their records on Victor's 35-cent Bluebird label were all hits. The first was the Miller theme, 'Moonlight Serenade', a tune he had written during his days with Ray Noble.

Miller followed up with 'Little Brown Jug', and during the summer of 1939 recorded an average of four sides every two weeks. 'In The Mood', Miller's biggest-selling record, was first offered to Artie Shaw. He liked it and played it often at concerts, but the arrangement was an eight-minute one, far too long for a record in those days. Determined to make it on record, the writer, Joe Garland, sent it to Miller who managed to fit it on to a single side by careful cutting. In the first two months of 1940 the band recorded thirty sides, including 'Tuxedo Junction'. Later came 'Pennsylvania Six-Five Thousand' (the phone number of a New York hotel where the band played), 'Chattanooga Choo-Choo' and a stream of hits that seemed never-ending.

On 27 September 1942, Miller stunned the music world by announcing that he was joining the armed forces. He didn't have to go, he was too old to be drafted. But he said: 'I have an obligation to fulfil, to lend as much support as I can to winning the war.' Perfectionist Miller took over the many top bandsmen who had been called up and rehearsed them hard, whipping them into shape for his American Air Force Band. He toured bases and broadcast coast-to-coast recruitment shows. In the spring of 1944, he and his men were posted to England, 'to bring a much-needed touch of home to some lads who have been starved for real, live American music'.

In less than twelve months overseas, the band made three hundred personal appearances and five hundred broadcasts. After England, they were scheduled to go to the Continent for six weeks. They were such a hit that they stayed for six months. But the man who had made the success possible was no longer there to enjoy it. On 15 December 1944, Major Glenn Miller took off with two companions in a small plane to fly to Paris to make final arrangements for the transfer of his troops to Europe. Neither he nor his companions were ever seen again, and no wreckage of the plane was ever found.

Harry James continued to struggle along for some time after losing Frank Sinatra to Tommy Dorsey. Then an astute suggestion from Columbia A & R man Morty Palitz turned him into one of the company's biggest money-spinners. The advice: cut down on the swing, and add some strings. James did just that. On 20 May 1941, he added his schmaltzy trumpet to the rich vocals of Dick Haymes on 'You Made Me Love You', and came up with a smash hit. Then he recorded with former Benny Goodman vocalist Helen Forrest, producing a series of titles tailored to the emotions of wartime – 'He's 1-A In The Army And He's A-1 In My Heart', 'I Don't Want To Walk Without You', 'He's My Guy' and 'That Soldier Of Mine'. Even James was staggered by the reaction. His band smashed attendance records all over the country, appearing on commercial radio five nights a week.

◄Florence Desmond, the Australian comedienne whose impersonations of well-known film stars brought her international fame.

Glenn Miller, here with Dinah Shore at Abbey Road Studios, volunteered his services to the US Forces when beyond draft age. Major Miller died in a plane crash while on his way to entertain the troops.

By 1942 James's success had become almost an embarrassment to Columbia: the company announced that it was running short of shellac to make more records. James's version of 'I've Heard That Song Before' had hit 1.25 million sales, the highest figure Columbia had ever had. 'Velvet Moon' and 'You Made Me Love You' had both passed a million, and the re-released 'All Or Nothing At All', featuring Sinatra's voice, had reached 975,000. (It had logged up just 16,000 sales the first time around.) That year, total record sales in America hit 140 million.

But James was losing interest in the big-band scene. Some blamed it on the counter-attractions of his beautiful new wife, actress Betty Grable. He continued to make money, but by 1946, when the supply of bands far outweighed demand, he decided to call it a day. He announced his decision in December, the same month that seven other leaders broke up their bands: Benny Goodman, Tommy Dorsey, Les Brown, Jack Teagarden, Benny Carter, Woody Herman and Ina Ray Hutton. Almost all of them would try again in later years as dance music and jazz drifted apart, and jazz fragmented into bebop, progressive and modern styles that took little account of popular taste. But they would never again reach the same dizzy heights. For the next twenty-five years, popular music in America belonged to the people the bandleaders had done so much to help – solo singers.

Europe, which followed the trends set by America, had no equivalent to the US swing bands. Optimism was at a premium in countries under the growing threat of fascism and war. In Britain, lovers of swing had to rely on records for their thrills. HMV issued a Benny Goodman series under the reciprocal agreements negotiated with Victor and Columbia USA years before. Ellington, Basie, Artie Shaw, Tommy Dorsey and Glenn Miller were all available on either HMV or Columbia.

But though American swing bands dominated the popular-music record market on both sides of the Atlantic, several British bands were finding success in their own fields. Joe Loss and Billy Cotton concentrated on the ballroom crowds rather than on London High Society, and the bands who had played the West End in its heyday were moving out in search of new audiences. Nat Gonella, a contemporary of Bowlly in Lew Stone's band, was one of many who had taken to the variety circuit, putting on a mixture of jazz, romantic crooning and visual comedy. Entertainment was the name of the game, and bands were expected to be self-contained variety shows.

They were taking over a role that had been filled by vaudeville artists. By the '30s, music-hall was dying, kept going only by the really big names: Gracie Fields, who recorded monster hits like 'Sally' and 'Now Is The Hour'; George Formby, whose cheeky lyrics led to comedy successes such as 'When I'm Cleaning Windows' and 'Leaning On The Lamp-post'; and Flanagan and Allen, who sold well for Columbia with 'Underneath The Arches' and 'Hometown'. But they, like other top attractions – 'Two ton' Tessie O'Shea, soliloquist Stanley Holloway, and Jack Buchanan and Cicely Courtneidge – were finding more lucrative outlets. Radio and the growing film industry were taking away the talent.

When war broke out again in Europe, the music industry again responded to the need to foster patriotism and maintain morale. Vera Lynn, who had been Bert Ambrose's band's singer, toured the country and service camps singing such tear-jerkers as 'We'll Meet

Vera Lynn, the Forces' Sweetheart during the Second World War, whose songs like
'We'll Meet Again' and ' The White Cliffs of Dover' epitomize the music of that period, went on to
establish herself as a recording artist and television performer of great style and distinction.

Again', 'There'll Always Be An England' and 'The White Cliffs Of Dover'. Her flag-waving visits to the front quickly earned her the rank of Forces' Sweetheart. Flanagan and Allen came up with a hit that made stiff upper lips smile: 'Run Rabbit, Run' was inspired by the news that the first German bomb to fall on the British Isles had killed a rabbit.

Much of the giant HMV Hayes record factory was turned over to the production of munitions, but there was still a big demand for discs. The company's catalogue included some extraordinary novelties. There was the notorious 'peace in our time' speech by Premier Neville Chamberlain after his meeting with Hitler in Munich, some 'cheeky chappie' patter from the Palladium by comedian Max Miller, and even an RAF label which offered, among other things, a recording of a bomber crew on a raid over Essen. Cynics said the language was too clean for the recording to be authentic.

British bands that had managed to keep working in London were now driven further afield by the Luftwaffe blitz. One leader, Ken 'Snakehips' Johnson, was killed with one of his musicians when a bomb hit the Café de Paris as they played. A month later, in April 1941, Al Bowlly, the singer who had left America just as vocalists were beginning to emerge as big stars, also died in an air-raid. He was almost penniless.

Ironically, however, the war provided Britain with its best swing band. Players from many bands had been called up into the RAF. They got together to entertain service personnel and became known as the Squadronaires. One critic described the band as 'the greatest thing in jazz this country has produced'. As well as touring the war spots, the band broadcast on the radio, recorded for Decca, and was used in propaganda shows beamed at German forces. The Squadronaires' forces rivals included the Skyrockets, a band from the No. 1 Balloon Centre at Kidbrooke, London, who recorded for Rex and Parlophone, and an Army outfit, the RAOC Blue Rockets, formed by conductor Eric Robinson, who were signed by HMV.

The Squadronaires stayed together after the war, finally breaking up in 1964. By then, Britain had found another band of international calibre. Ted Heath, who had been a trombonist with Jack Hylton and Bert Ambrose before the war, and had played with Geraldo's band during it, formed an orchestra of his own in 1944, offering jobs to several of the service bandsmen. He began a series of Swing Sessions at the London Palladium, accompanying visiting stars such as Ella Fitzgerald, and discovering a talented line-up of home-grown singers, Dickie Valentine, Lita Rosa and Dennis Lotis. In 1956 he became the first British band leader to tour America as part of an exchange that brought Stan Kenton to Britain.

But Heath was the last of a dying breed, a reminder of the golden pre-war big-band days. Now, on both sides of the Atlantic, solo singers were getting all the attention. In America, the overlapping of the eras was summed up in a poignant TV scene. The ageing Dorsey brothers took a break from playing their music to introduce a fresh-faced young hopeful who was getting his first big break. His name was Elvis Presley.

Herbert von Karajan, was the first new German artist signed by E.M.I. after the war. He became one of the legends of the postwar period, creating in the process a huge catalogue of recordings.

CLASSICS DILEMMAS

Austerity and the ration book ruled as war-weary Britain picked up the pieces after six years of fighting. But at prestige-conscious E.M.I. it was still a case of 'only the best will do'. Working for the company was considered an honour, and all male staff, even artists, were expected to wear suits and ties. At Abbey Road, studio engineers wore crisp white jackets – and woe betide any musician who dared to loosen his tie during a recording session.

An organization so confident of its 'By Appointment' status and superiority could have only one philosophy when it came to rebuilding its classical catalogue: the greatest artists were to be represented by their finest performances, so giving classical recording a new Golden Age.

In 1946, E.M.I.'s two senior classical music producers (the legendary Fred Gaisberg having retired) Walter Legge and David Bicknell set off around Europe to seek out and sign those artists.

Travelling across a continent so recently ravaged by war was far from easy. Bicknell arrived at Amsterdam to find the airport still in ruins. He hitched a bizarre lift into town, sitting on a pile of mangel-wurzels in a trailer that was attached to a lorry powered by a wheezing charcoal-burner.

In Vienna, where the famous State Opera House had been reduced to rubble by bombs, Legge contacted Wilhelm Furtwängler, conductor of the Berlin Philharmonic, and

drew up a new recording contract. Performances of the State Opera were being staged in the Theater an der Wein, and there Legge heard the soprano Elisabeth Schwarzkopf. He was to fall in love with her and make her his wife – after signing her for Columbia. Legge's quest for artists was thwarted only once. After a concert by the Vienna Philharmonic under Otto Klemperer, he pushed his way backstage to try to recruit the conductor, only to find that he had signed for a rival label. It was 1954 before Klemperer finally recorded for E.M.I.

Also in Vienna at that time was a young, up-and-coming conductor called Herbert von Karajan. He had been considered by E.M.I.'s German company before the war but rejected with the comment: 'The artist will not reach international class.' Now Legge signed him – and immediately fell foul of Furtwängler, who threatened to tear up his own contract unless von Karajan was dropped. Bicknell was ordered to Vienna to help sort out the problem, and in the end a compromise was arranged which soothed Furtwängler sufficiently for him to stay with E.M.I., but the bitterness between the two eminent conductors continued for years.

While Legge concentrated on Vienna, Bicknell based himself in Rome. Soon after arriving (on a military plane), he called at the luxurious villa owned by Gigli, and found the great singer sitting in his garden, ready and willing to start recording again. The many Allied soldiers still in Italy had developed a liking for opera, thanks to the free tickets offered by the Rome Opera House, and Bicknell decided to cash in on this potential market. Gigli agreed to record *Aida*, with a superb supporting cast including Ebe Stignani, Maria Caniglia and Gino Bechi, and Bicknell also arranged for *La Traviata* to be recorded and released on a cheap label for the troops. Recording equipment was shipped out from London in dozens of crates and, despite all the difficulties posed by such an ambitious project so soon after the war, both operas were on disc and in the shops before the end of 1946.

Even though E.M.I. had now been in existence for fifteen years, the separate identities of the Columbia and HMV labels were still jealously preserved. Both Legge and Bicknell had *carte blanche* to pursue independent programmes and, because there was little consultation between them, they were sometimes recording the same works at the same time in different parts of Europe. When Columbia's Legge was producing Beethoven's Fifth with von Karajan in Vienna, HMV's Bicknell was recording the identical symphony with Sir John Barbirolli at Abbey Road. While Bicknell was working on Debussy's *La Mer* in Rome with Victor de Sabata, Legge was recording it with Galliera and the Philharmonia in London. Nobody at E.M.I. thought it odd that these records should be in direct competition when they reached the shops.

There were those who took pride in the continual battle between HMV and Columbia to produce the best classical recordings, and the duplication of great works became even more apparent during the mid '50s. By then, E.M.I. and its associated companies in the United States had virtually all the world's leading classical artists under contract. They had the best conductors: Barbirolli, Beecham, Boult, Cantelli, Furtwängler, Klemperer,

◄ Wilhelm Furtwängler, conductor of the Berlin Philharmonic had been signed to HMV before the war. An outspoken foe of Hitler and the Nazi philosophy, he had found himself without an orchestra. Yet his genius had remained and he returned to his earlier brilliance as a conductor, especially for the record.

Ormandy, Sargent, Stokowski, Toscanini, von Karajan. They had the best pianists: Arrau, Horowitz, Lipatti, Michelangeli, Rubinstein, Solomon. They had the best violinists: Heifetz, Menuhin, Stern, Szigeti. They had· the best singers: Callas, Christoff, de los· Angeles, di Stefano, Gigli, Gobbi, Schwarzkopf . . . They had the best of everything. For a company intent on maintaining its prestige, it looked impressive to have forty-five conductors under contract. But from a commercial point of view, that total was a little ludicrous. Such excesses had gone unchecked partly because the E.M.I. directors had more serious matters on their minds. . .potentially far more disastrous than a surfeit of top talent.

Sir Ernest Fisk, an Australian electronics expert, had been appointed E.M.I. Managing Director in 1945 and had started an orgy of reorganization which produced great acrimony in the boardroom. Fisk was not too interested in recording. He had eyes only for the golden future of the electronics business. His first major project was to produce a cheap television set which turned out to be so shoddy and unreliable that HMV's high reputation in the marketplace was seriously undermined. Exclusive HMV dealerships had been bestowed on the basis of one per town and were highly prized, a mark of considerable standing in the trade. Under Fisk, shop owners were actually offering to relinquish their franchises – an unheard-of thing – rather than be saddled with some of the products emerging from Hayes.

Another enormous problem was the products that were *not* emerging from Hayes. In June 1948, Columbia Records of America held a press conference at New York's Waldorf Astoria to announce a 'revolutionary new product' – the long-playing record. The microgroove disc, revolving at a speed of only $33\frac{1}{3}$ r.p.m., was the exciting breakthrough classical music had been waiting for. Listening to a complete symphony on the old 78 r.p.m. records meant constantly having to change sides and discs and, no matter how ingenious the studio producer was, breaks often came at the most inopportune moments. The LP, which lasted twenty-three minutes per side, gave music enthusiasts the chance to enjoy entire movements without interruption. Columbia's rivals, RCA–Victor, spent $5 million on advertising, trying to fight the LP with its 'bookshelf size' seven-inch records, which revolved at 45 r.p.m. and were more convenient and compact than 78s. But it conceded defeat early in 1950, and began issuing a classical repertoire on its own 'new and improved' LPs. By the middle of the year, 78 r.p.m. shellac records were a thing of the past in America, used only. for a few dance-tunes.

Incredibly, none of these fundamental changes made any impression on Sir Ernest Fisk. When E.M.I. artists asked when they could expect to start recording LPs, the word from the boardroom was that Fisk could see 'no future for the long-playing record'. It was not a view shared by E.M.I.'s major competitor, Decca. It began issuing LPs early in 1950, and several top E.M.I. artists soon followed the example of the D'Oyly Carte Company, which switched to Decca to take advantage of the new disc speed. E.M.I. waited until 1952 before deciding to enter the LP market.

Otto Klemperer, the German conductor, whose career blossomed after the Second World War despite a series of accidents and illnesses. He overcame adversity to produce in the last two decades of his life a legacy of great recorded performances with the Philharmonia Orchestra, including a set of Beethoven Symphonies which stand as a monument to his art.▶

Sir Adrian Boult, the premier latterday British conductor and Dame Janet Baker, a British singer of distinction and accomplishment, collaborated on a number of projects including Brahms: Alto Rhapsody and Wagner: Wesendonck Songs.

Sir William Walton

Sir John Barbirolli

Victoria de los Angeles, Spain's great lady of song for over three decades, recorded more than twenty complete operas and twenty-five recital recordings for E.M.I.

A third headache for the E.M.I. board was the steadily deteriorating relations with the company's American partners. Both RCA-Victor and Columbia were baffled by how E.M.I.'s competing labels worked, and both were increasingly convinced that they were getting the worse of the transatlantic exchange deal. David Sarnoff, president of RCA-Victor, visited Hayes in 1951 to discuss the arrangement and was far from impressed by what he found. He was kept waiting an hour because the chairman was late – which gave him plenty of time to notice the run-down state of the offices. Dirty windows and holes in the linoleum covering miles of corridors were symptoms of a once-great company going down-hill. When Sir Ernest Fisk was forced to resign at the end of 1951, E.M.I. was in a perilous financial position.

News of the impending break with the two American record giants caused alarm in the classical music departments of both HMV and Columbia. Many of the great artists originally signed by E.M.I. had stayed in the United States after the war and transferred to RCA-Victor or to Columbia for the sake of administrative convenience. If the record-exchange deal ended, E.M.I. stood to lose dozens of top stars of the calibre of Rubinstein, Heifetz, Toscanini, Horowitz, Milanov and Björling. A crash programme of recording was implemented to build up the E.M.I. catalogue before the split and a new company, Angel Records, was launched for the US market. At La Scala, Milan, fifteen complete operas were recorded between 1953 and 1955, supplemented by others in Rome, London and elsewhere. When the transatlantic break finally came, HMV was left with Beecham, de los Angeles and Menuhin; Columbia had von Karajan, Klemperer, Schwarzkopf and – most precious of all – Maria Callas.

Walter Legge first heard Callas sing in Bellini's *Norma* at the Rome Opera in the summer of 1951. He was electrified by her performance, and rushed backstage to offer her an exclusive recording contract. Both Callas and her manager-husband, Giovanni Meneghini, seemed delighted by the offer, but neither was ready to rush into an agreement, particularly since she was already recording for the Italian Cetra label. Negotiations dragged on for months, with Legge always arriving at their Verona apartment with some gift for the diva. 'My arms still ache at the recollection of the pots of flowering shrubs and trees I lugged to their door,' he recalled. When terms were at last agreed, Legge signed the contract on behalf of E.M.I., only to be told that Callas could not put her name to it for two weeks, as she had a superstition about not signing agreements immediately. Meneghini promised that the contract would be put in the post, but it failed to arrive. Legge returned to Verona and found that Meneghini wanted more money. It was July 1952 before Callas at last became an E.M.I. recording artist.

The sensational records she provided made the long and wearisome process of capturing her thoroughly worthwhile. Her *Tosca*, recorded with Tito Gobbi and Giuseppe di Stefano, conducted by Victor de Sabata and produced by Legge at La Scala in 1953 remains one of the most celebrated classical recordings of all time. It took eleven exhausting days to make, with all the principals determined to seek perfection. Gobbi sang his First Act part thirty times before he was satisfied, and Callas worked on a single six-word phrase for half an hour before she was ready to include it in her performance.

Not all her recording sessions were marked by such dedicated professionalism. If things were not going well, she was liable to turn in a fury on the producer, conductor, orchestra, engineers or anyone else who happened to cross her path. She was a difficult and demanding woman but a great artist, and she was always forgiven. E.M.I. once threw an expensive party for her in New York, inviting a glittering list of celebrities – but Maria failed to turn up. On another occasion, Marlene Dietrich was worried about Callas's health as she rehearsed for an opera appearance. The German star spent hours boiling a broth from eight pounds of beef. Maria thanked her profusely. 'It was wonderful,' she said. 'Tell me, what brand of cubes do you use?'

Callas's brilliant E.M.I. recording career ended unhappily. In 1968 she agreed to attempt once more the fiendishly difficult role of La Traviata. Producer Peter Andry, intent on an historic record, put together the finest cast he could assemble for the Rome sessions. Conductor Carlo Maria Giulini agreed to give up three weeks of his time, Luciano Pavarotti was engaged to sing opposite the diva – after she had objected to Placido Domingo – and the smaller roles and chorus were all lined up. Then, a week before the day recording was due to start, Maria told Andry by phone that she was backing out because Rome was 'too cold' in September. 'The truth was that she had lost her nerve,' Andry said later, 'but of course she would never admit it. It was one of the biggest disappointments in my life. Giulini never forgave her and never spoke to her again.' Andry, however, did not bear a grudge. The next

Sir Thomas Beecham had become the giant of recent British musical history. He set standards which remain unsurpassed and his legacy of recordings covers standard repertoire, rare titles and operas, of which *Carmen* and *La Bohème*, both with Victoria de los Angeles, must be considered superb examples of Beecham's best work.

Tito Gobbi (left), one of the finest singing actors of the century. During the 1950s Gobbi recorded a series of operas, mainly at La Scala and the Rome Opera House, in which his unrivalled assumptions of the leading baritone roles such as Rigoletto, Scarpia, Falstaff and Gianni Schichi remain the standard against which all subsequent performers are judged.

Jussi Björling (right), the Swedish tenor, made his first records under the assumed name of Eric Odde, singing with a dance band for Swedish HMV. He went on to become one of the world's most successful and best loved opera singers and made many fine recordings, of which his Rudolfo in *La Bohème* with Victoria de los Angeles and Sir Thomas Beecham is one of the treasures of the gramophone.

◄ Boris Christoff, the Bulgarian bass, is regarded by many as the successor to Chaliapin. Like his great predecessor, Christoff's most successful operatic role is Mussorgsky's Boris Godunov which he recorded in two definitive performances for E.M.I. in 1952 and, in stereo, in 1962.

time Callas telephoned him, it was to ask if he could get her a discount on a television she wanted to buy. They bantered about it and, when she died in Paris in 1977, Andry was one of the pallbearers at her funeral.

Maria Callas was not the only star whose tantrums and whims caused sleepless nights for busy record producers. One careless comment or imagined slight could ruin in a second sessions carefully planned for months. Di Stefano once swept out of a Florence studio after the conductor gently suggested he was singing in F-natural instead of F-sharp. The great tenor left without a word and caught the first train home to Bologna, leaving the conductor, orchestra and studio staff wondering how to fill the rest of the day.

In 1953, HMV lost the great Wagnerian soprano Kirsten Flagstad. She was due to record *Tristan und Isolde* with Furtwängler conducting, but difficult negotiations with the conductor had dragged on for months. During lunch one day with David Bicknell, the singer confessed: 'There is one note I cannot sing now; if Furtwängler waits much longer, there will be two.' Flagstad was not joking. Then nearly sixty years old, she could not reach top C. When the session was finally arranged, Elisabeth Schwarzkopf was secretly smuggled into the studio to sing the top notes for her. The result was a superb recording, and everyone was happy – until the story somehow leaked to the newspapers. Humiliated, the furious Flagstad walked out on HMV and joined Decca.

Tempers again flared when Victoria de los Angeles, normally even-tempered, was recording *Carmen* in Paris with Sir Thomas Beecham in 1955. The session had not gone well from the start. Sir Thomas, then seventy-six, was tired and irritable after a long concert tour, and relations between him and the soprano grew more and more strained. Finally, de los Angeles telephoned David Bicknell at his home in England, and said she could not stand it a moment longer – she was going home to Barcelona. Bicknell begged her to wait until he could get to Paris to sort matters out, but she would agree to meet him only briefly at the airport. He caught the first available flight and found her waiting at Orly. She refused absolutely to reconsider and stunned Bicknell by revealing that she had not told Beecham she was leaving. Bicknell drove straight to the Ritz Hotel and knocked at the door of Sir Thomas's suite. The maestro appeared wearing baggy blue trousers, red braces and a silk shirt. 'Where's Carmen?' he demanded. 'Just touching down at Barcelona airport, I should imagine,' Bicknell replied. Beecham flew into a rage. At that moment a waiter backed in through the doors with a lunch no one had ordered. 'All Tommy's wrath burst on this poor fellow's head, first in French, then in English,' Bicknell recalled. 'I simply could not stop myself from bursting out laughing.' It took a year to patch up the differences between Beecham and de los Angeles, and to finish the recording. It was enormously successful.

Beecham was always a great favourite at Abbey Road, as much for his sparkling wit and lively personality as for his talents as a conductor. His recording sessions were often chaotic because he was constantly wanting to polish up previous performances. He would ask the orchestra to play a few bars from the last movement of Beethoven's Seventh, then a section

◄Maria Callas, the Greek-born soprano, was undoubtedly both the greatest and the most temperamental star to appear on the opera scene after the war. After a difficult beginning, her recording career produced a glorious series of complete operas, many made at La Scala, Milan, which have become classics of the gramophone, including the legendary *Tosca* conducted by Victor de Sabata. Here she is recording *Norma* at Abbey Road.

of Sibelius, then Mozart, then Haydn. It was a nightmare for the recording engineers, for the balance on each work would be different. But if they tried to explain their problems to Beecham, he wickedly pretended not to understand. Sometimes he would change his mind at the last moment as to what to record. If he did not feel like conducting the Mozart symphony scheduled for a particular day, he would ask the Abbey Road librarian, 'What else have we got in the old oak chest?' and choose anything that took his fancy. Nobody else but 'Tommy' could have got away with it.

Another real character on the E.M.I. roster was Italian pianist Arturo Benedetti Michelangeli. Peter Andry recalled having to chase him round Europe for sessions: 'Someone would ring up and say the maestro was ready to record. So I would go to Italy and find he was somewhere else. I would follow him to Switzerland and be told he was in bed and wouldn't see me. I would wait two days and he would be rude and refuse to discuss recording. Eventually he would agree a date and I would book an orchestra, then he wouldn't turn up.' Michelangeli, a perfectionist about music, was never satisfied with the tone of his instrument. Andry often found him poised angrily over his piano, the insides of which would be scattered around the room, while a Japanese tuner filed furiously at the felts to try to improve the sound. When at long last Michelangeli arrived at Abbey Road to record Ravel's Piano Concerto and Rachmaninoff's Fourth, the session was delayed for three hours while he and his tuner dismantled and re-assembled the piano half a dozen times. But the record that resulted, one of only three completed with Michaelangeli during his twenty-five years with the company, was superb.

In 1955, E.M.I. reclaimed its position as the trend-setter of the European musical scene by issuing the first stereo recordings on 7½ i.p.s. tape. Stereo discs from E.M.I. first appeared in 1958. The two-channel system of sound had been discovered twenty-four years earlier by a young scientist working in the company's Hayes laboratories. Alan Blumlein, an electronics genius, was hired by Columbia in 1929, at the age of twenty-six, to redesign the recording system then in use, and within twelve months he came up with a much improved process offering better frequency response and less distortion. A year later, Blumlein was experimenting with stereophonic sound – he called it binaural reproduction – and in December he filed Patent 394325. But though E.M.I. scientists continued to work on the idea over the years, excessive surface noise caused by the cutting of the master record prevented commercial use. It was not until the mid '50s, after the arrival of magnetic tape for recording, that all the technical problems were finally ironed out.

The record-buying public found the exciting new advance a revelation. Stereo liberated recorded sound, bringing the concert-hall into the home with a realism, depth and breadth never previously experienced. But the genius who had pioneered the breakthrough was not around to hear his ideas put into practice. Alan Blumlein registered more than 120 patents for technological innovations in recording, wireless and television before going to work with other boffins to develop radar when the 1939–45 war broke out. On 7 June 1942, a

Elvira in *I Puritani*

Tosca

Rosina in *Barber of Seville*

Medea

Turandot

Norma

Carmen

Madame Butterfly

Violetta in *La Traviata*

Halifax bomber in which he was testing equipment crashed in the south of England and everyone on board was killed instantaneously.

Stereo enhanced all forms of music, but operatic recordings in particular gained enormously. In *Madame Butterfly*, Victoria de los Angeles could be *heard* climbing the hill to the house where Pinkerton awaited her. When *Boris Godunov* was re-recorded in stereo in 1962 the great dramatic bass Boris Christoff performed the extraordinary feat of singing three separate roles: the title role, the monk Pimen and the cameo part of the ruffian Varlaam in the inn scene. Christoff, signed by Legge in the '40s, ranked with Tito Gobbi as one of the finest singer-actors ever seen on the operatic stage. Especially memorable was their performance together at Covent Garden as King Philip and Rodrigo in Visconti's *Don Carlos*, where they repeated roles of electrifying dramatic power which had already been vividly recorded for E.M.I.

In 1964 Walter Legge retired after an extraordinary career during which he had discovered, nurtured and encouraged countless artists, building them into top international stars. He was a perfectionist, unwilling to compromise, always seeking the ultimate performance, and his contribution to classical recording was second only to that of the pioneer, Fred Gaisberg. After Legge left the Columbia label, the classical catalogue was concentrated on HMV, a rationalization which was long overdue.

But even this move did not always prevent embarrassing duplication of works. In the summer of 1968, a curious chain of events presented HMV with two sets of the complete Beethoven piano concertos, finished within a month of each other. For some time, E.M.I. had been trying to persuade Otto Klemperer to conduct the Beethoven works, but he could never decide which soloist he wanted. Despairing of ever being able to satisfy Klemperer, HMV arranged to record the concerts with soloist Emil Gilels and the Cleveland Orchestra conducted by George Szell. No sooner had this deal been signed than Klemperer conducted a Mozart concerto with the New Philharmonia and a young pianist called Daniel Barenboim. Immediately afterwards, Klemperer announced that Barenboim, a former child prodigy, was the soloist he had been looking for. He was now ready to record the Beethoven piano concertos. HMV arranged the session and it proved a great success. Barenboim went on to become a prolific recording artist, both as pianist and conductor.

Another Beethoven record, issued by HMV late in 1969, is still rated one of the finest classical recordings ever made. The Triple Concerto brought together the Berlin Philharmonic under von Karajan and three celebrated Russian soloists, cellist Mstislav Rostropovich, pianist Sviatoslav Richter and violinist Igor Oistrakh. Its musical brilliance represented a triumph of organization and perseverance for Peter Andry. He had pursued von Karajan for years to make the record, but the maestro could never find the time. Apart from being musical director of the Berlin Philharmonic, he was also conductor of the Vienna State Opera, the Salzburg Festival and Milan's La Scala. Von Karajan was once said to have rushed out of a concert-hall into a taxi. When the driver asked, 'Where to?' he replied:

◄Callas as Norma. The photo shows Callas at her best; a great beauty, a striking personality and a fine actress.

'It doesn't matter, I have engagements everywhere.'

Because of that busy schedule, only three sessions were available for the Triple Concerto recording in Berlin, and von Karajan missed the first. He arrived for the seond an hour and a half late, played a few bars, then angrily insisted that the entire orchestra change positions. The three soloists were far from pleased by the delay, but von Karajan's power was absolute – if he wanted something changed, it had to be changed. Every one of 110 musicians was moved, along with all the recording equipment . . . which wasted most of the second session. On the third and last day, time was so short that it seemed the recording could never be completed. But the orchestra and soloists played to almost miraculous perfection, and created a milestone in classical recording: the sale of one million discs.

Classical record-makers and musicians had always considered themselves a race apart from popular music and the masses who supported it. But in the '60s, classical recordings suddenly and unexpectedly began to capture the attention and interest of a much wider public. The London Symphony Orchestra's version of Rachmaninoff's Second Symphony, conducted by André Previn, took everyone at HMV completely by surprise when it became a phenomenal best-seller. Previn's jazz collaboration with violinist Itzhak Perlman was similarly successful. They had recorded many violin concertos together, but Perlman was anxious to try his hand at a different discipline. He explained: 'Knowing André's affinity for the jazz idiom, I finally gathered all the *chutzpah* I could find, called him up and asked if he would collaborate in a jazz recording. I think he was rather flabbergasted but, recovering quickly, he agreed.'

Another astonishing seller was an album called *West Meets East*, featuring Yehudi Menuhin on violin and Ravi Shankar on sitar. Shankar had recorded for HMV in India for several years, but he was almost unknown in the West until the Beatles took an interest in his music. The idea for the *West Meets East* album came from Air India, who commissioned the recording privately from E.M.I. as a sales promotion – they planned to give it away to first-class passengers. When budget cutbacks forced the airline to pull out of the deal after the record had been made, HMV decided to cut its losses by issuing the album independently. Nobody expected much interest, but sales took off, both in Europe and America, until the LP was soaring up the pop charts.

It was a sign of the new times which both Menuhin and Perlman, by many considered to be the finest violinists of the past fifty years, understood and felt drawn to. The pop Top Twenty now dominated the recorded-music business all over the world. In the old days, E.M.I. might have been tempted to ignore that fact and continue doggedly down the heavily classical track. Luckily, the company had a man at the top more attuned to the trends of the marketplace. And when the pop explosion came, E.M.I. was ready for it.

◄ Yehudi Menuhin, thirty years on and still among the world's finest violinists, now experimented with new musical expressions. He recorded and played with jazz musicians and his collaboration with Ravi Shankar on sitar, an album called *West Meets East*, became a smash hit on the 'pop' as opposed to the classical charts.

After lengthy negotiations and diplomatic manoeuvres, E.M.I. managed to bring the great Russian performers to London for recording sessions. Above: an exuberant Rostropovich, below: a gloomy trio of Lev Oborin (piano), David Oistrakh (violin) and Sviatoslav Kushnevitzky (cello) listen to a replay of their recording, joined by producer Walter Jellinek on left.

◄Dmitri Shostakovich, the Soviet composer, was acclaimed a major composer at twenty after the sensational premièr of his First Symphony. However, the development of his musical thought brought him into difficulties with the Soviet authorities and his reply was the most popular of all twentieth-century symphonies, his Fifth.

André Previn is one of the most versatile of today's classical musicians. As conductor, composer and pianist he has covered every aspect of music from classical to film scores, television themes and jazz, and his many recordings, especially those with the London Symphony Orchestra, have been highly successful.

The violinists Itzakh Perlman and Pinchas Zukerman and the conductor/pianist Daniel Barenboim are leading superstars of the new generation of classical recording. Here they are collaborating on a recording of Bach's Violin Concertos.

The Italian conductor Carlo Maria Giulini has made many of his finest recordings for E.M.I. Renowned for his sensitive musicianship and depth of musical feeling, he is especially noted for his interpretation of Verdi's Requiem, and his recording of this work with the Philharmonia Orchestra and Chorus is a masterpiece.

Riccardo Muti is one of today's busiest and most important conductors. His regular appointments include the Maggio Musicale in Florence, the Philadelphia Orchestra and the Philharmonia in London as well as guest appearances at major international festivals and opera houses. An exclusive EMI recording artist, he has already won several important awards for his varied and extensive achievements on record including a number of operas by Verdi and orchestral works by Stravinsky, Tchaikovsky, Mendelssohn and Schumann amongst others.

CROONERS & SWOONERS

Crossing America by train shortly after the 1939–45 war, Sir Thomas Beecham was delighted to discover milling crowds of young people at every station, waiting, he presumed, to catch a glimpse of him. Only when they failed to acknowledge his regal waves did the suspicion dawn on the great man that he might not be the object of their adoring attention. Could someone even more famous be travelling on the same train? Sir Thomas made discreet enquiries which revealed a fellow-passenger who came from the dockyard city of Hoboken, New Jersey – a crooner by the name of Frank Sinatra.

If the classical conductor was mystified by all the fuss, it was entirely understandable. No entertainer had ever generated the kind of mass hysteria which surrounded Sinatra. Adolescent bobbysoxers screamed and swooned at his voice, fought like tigers to be near him, touch his hand, rip a piece from his jacket, wrench a lock of hair from his head. The newspapers were full of this curious new teenage phenomenon. Headlines shrieked about 'Swoonatra' and 'Sinatraddicts'. When he appeared at New York's Paramount Theatre in 1944, 10,000 fans stood, six abreast, in a queue that stretched west along 43rd Street, trailed down Eighth Avenue, and wound east up 44th Street. Another 20,000 teenagers jammed Times Square, bringing cars and pedestrians to a halt. Popular music had generated the first of a new breed of stars – the sex symbol.

Sinatra led the way for solo singers as the big bands who had dominated the previous decade begin to decline. He left Tommy Dorsey in September 1942 and was soon the heart-throb of a generation of young girls, the vocal substitute for boyfriends and husbands posted abroad in the war. Inspired by his success, other band singers struck out on their own: Perry Como, Rosemary Clooney, Jo Stafford, Peggy Lee, Dinah Shore. But none could match Ol' Blue Eyes, as he later became known. Bing Crosby once said: 'Frank Sinatra is the kind of singer who comes along once in a lifetime – but why did it have to be mine?' In fact, but for Bing, Frank Sinatra might never have come along.

◄ The first singer to leave the big bands, Frank Sinatra left Tommy Dorsey in 1942 to become a solo singer. He became more than that, an instant heart-throb to a generation of young girls who fainted at the sight of him. He went on to become the most durable voice, and a legend.

Crosby had been the first of the big-band vocalists to make it as a solo artist, and for thirteen years had had the field to himself. Born Harry Lillis Crosby in 1901, he was re-christened by schoolmates at Spokane, Washington, because of his obsession with a comic strip called the Bingville Bugle. Working in the props department of the local theatre provided him with what he called 'the first priming coat of show-business', and an early wind-up gramophone settled his destiny.

As his father brought home all the latest popular tunes of the day, Bing sang and whistled them as he walked round the town. 'Everybody in Spokane knew when I was coming by,' he recalled. 'I had a constant succession of tunes in my head, and I had to get them out.' The family sent him to study law at Gonzaga University, but Bing was more interested in hits than writs. He formed a singing group with his pal, Al Rinker, to entertain fellow students, and together they decided to make music their career. After absorbing vaudeville and jazz influences, they were hired by bandleader Paul Whiteman for his vocal trio, the Rhythm Boys.

Soon their snappy presentation made them the big attraction at concerts, and records such as 'Mississippi Mud' sold well. Bing's distinctive solo spots became more and more popular, and in 1929 he broke from the band to record 'My Kinda Love' and 'Till We Meet' on his own. Two years later, the success of 'I Surrender Dear' led to network radio exposure, a five-nights-a-week fifteen-minute spot on CBS. For the next ten years he was unique – a solo singer in the golden age of big bands, the only vocalist who could challenge them in the record sales charts and command star billing for concerts. He played New York's Paramount Theatre, and began making a series of Hollywood movies which provided even more hit records – 'Easy To Remember', 'Temptation', 'Pennies From Heaven', and 'Swinging On A Star', from *Going My Way*.

Crosby played down his ability. 'Honestly, I think I've stretched a talent which is so thin it's almost transparent over a quite unbelievable term of years,' he once said. 'Every man who sees one of my movies or who listens to my records or who hears me on the radio, believes firmly that he sings as well as I do, especially in the bathroom. I have none of the mannerisms of a trained singer and I have very little voice.' But there was enough of those rich, chocolate-brown tones to sell a staggering 300 million discs, at least thirty million of them his version of 'White Christmas', recorded in 1942 but dusted off and re-issued almost every year after that. There were enough mannerisms in the Old Groaner's relaxed style to inspire Andy Williams, Tony Bennett and Dean Martin, among others. And there was enough inspiration in his 'nice-and-easy does it' approach to turn Francis Albert Sinatra from a one-time truck-loader and newspaper copyboy into the first pop idol.

Sinatra, born in 1915, was the son of a Sicilian father and a Genoan mother. As a youngster he had virtually no interest in music, and radio and record stars made little impression on him. But one night he took his girlfriend Nancy Barbato – later to be the first of his four wives – to a Jersey City vaudeville theatre to see Crosby. 'He performed on stage

◀ Nat 'King' Cole, jazz pianist and singer, was signed by the new label, Capitol Records, in 1943. Well known in Hollywood nightspots as a vocalist, his smooth, smoky and incredibly sexy voice and leisurely timing soon catapulted him to stardom. At one point Cole was responsible for fully a quarter of all Capitol's income.

Peggy Lee

Sinatra spent the next two years entering talent contests and singing wherever and whenever he could: clubs, cafés, dances – until he got his first big break as a singer with Harry James's band. While he was carving out a career for himself on the East Coast of America, three people who were to have a big influence on him in the future were setting off on their own adventure out west. Capitol Records was set up in Los Angeles in 1942 by songwriter Johnny Mercer, film producer Buddy De Sylva and record retailer Glenn Wallichs, with an original investment of only $10,000. Two early successes, Mercer's 'Strip Polka', and 'Cow Cow Boogie' by Ella Mae Morse, helped establish the company, then, in 1943, Capitol signed a young black pianist and vocalist called Nat 'King' Cole. He had formed his own jazz trio, and was in great demand in the Hollywood nightspots, but it was as a singer that he made his first hit records, with numbers like 'Sweet Lorraine', 'It's Only A Paper Moon' and 'Route 66'. Cole had no problems finding new material. Amateur songwriters, anxious to get their material recorded, popped up in the most unexpected places. Once a deputy sheriff flagged down the trio's speeding bus in Oklahoma. Instead of handing out a traffic ticket, he produced a song he wanted Nat to sing.

Another time, a young man arrived at the Million Dollar Theatre in Los Angeles where Cole and his trio were rehearsing. Undaunted by the cool reception he met, Eden Ahbez returned again and again, offering fifty per cent of the rights of his song to anyone who could persuade Nat to sing it. Months later, Cole came across Ahbez's soiled music-sheet during a Capitol recording session, and tried the tune out. When he finished, there was a stunned silence in the control booth. 'What's the matter?' Nat asked. 'Unless I miss my guess,' said

The vocal quality of this velvet-voiced lady has made her a legend of her own time. Her biggest single success to date, is 'Fever' which reached No. 5 in the UK and No. 8 in the US charts.

Jim Conkling, the man in charge of the session, 'that will be the biggest piece of material I've ever heard. Where in the world did you get it?' Cole could remember only that the song came from a 'goofy-looking' guy named Eden Ahbez. Capitol began a frantic hunt for him, to buy the rights to his work. Calls to the musicians' union and song publishers drew a blank, but the police knew someone answering Ahbez's description living rough up in the Hollywood Hills. He was eventually discovered, in a sleeping bag, under one of the Ls of the big hillside HOLLYWOOD sign. A few months later, Nat King Cole's recording of 'Nature Boy' was broadcast on Station WNEW in New York. Within minutes, the station switchboard was jammed with inquiries. The song won Cole his first gold disc, and established him as a major international artist. Massive follow-up hits like 'Mona Lisa' and 'Too Young' soon meant that he was responsible for a quarter of Capitol's total sales.

Capitol branched out into country music and rhythm and blues in 1948. The major record companies, still based in New York, were caught napping as Capitol captured the top names in the then underrated styles: Tex Ritter, Wanda Jackson, Merle Travis and an ex-disc-jockey called Tennessee Ernie Ford. Ford's biggest hit, 'Sixteen Tons', was written by Travis, who used a phrase often uttered by his father, a Kentucky coalminer, for the immortal line: 'I owe my soul to the company store.' Ford later teamed up with jazz singer Kay Starr to make the country charts with 'I'll Never Be Free'. And Kay Starr herself reached the No. 1 spot in 1956 with 'Rock 'n' Roll Waltz'.

By the early '50s, Capitol's roster of artists included more big names: Peggy Lee, Dean Martin, Stan Kenton and Anita O'Day. Al Martino, an ex-bricklayer who had been encouraged to take up singing by Mario Lanza, was signed, and topped both the American and British hit parades in 1952 with 'Here In My Heart'. Guitarist Les Paul and his vocalist wife Mary Ford came up with a series of highly original million-selling hits, among them 'Mockin' Bird Hill', 'How High The Moon' and 'The World Is Waiting For The Sunrise'. Paul, who started out in a hillbilly band, had invented the solid-body electric guitar in 1941 while in hospital after a car crash.

In 1953, Glenn Wallichs pulled off a major coup for the rapidly expanding company. He persuaded Frank Sinatra to switch from Columbia to Capitol. At the time, Sinatra's dazzling career was going through a bad patch. He had divorced his first wife Nancy, mother of his three children, and was involved in a much-publicized pursuit of fiery screen star Ava Gardner. Worse, his voice was showing signs of wear. But Wallichs knew what he was doing. He paid off the singer's debts and teamed him with Nelson Riddle — a combination which was to produce one of the world's best-loved, best-selling pop-music albums, *Songs For Swinging Lovers*. Sinatra completed the most famous comeback in show-business by winning a gold disc for his hit 'Young At Heart', and an Oscar for his acting performance as Private Maggio in the film, *From Here To Eternity*. Between 1953 and 1961, rated by many critics as his most creative and satisfying period, he recorded 250 titles for Capitol.

Record sales in the United States rose from $189 million a year to $277 million between 1950 and 1955, largely because of the success of solo singers. RCA and Decca competed fiercely for the top artists and best songs, but it was Columbia who won the battle of the Big Three companies. Its glittering array of talent – Frankie Laine, Johnny Ray, Guy Mitchell, Doris Day, Rosemary Clooney – virtually took it in turns to follow one another to the top of the charts. Johnny Ray's famous million-seller, 'Cry', stayed at No. 1 for eleven weeks in 1952, despite fierce criticism of his style. The British *Melody Maker* magazine described his 'excruciating formula' of breaking into tears while singing as 'uninhibited and tasteless showmanship', and added: 'If an artist has to descend to this level to capture the masses, then the outlook for popular music is bleak indeed.' It was not a view shared by the record companies, who were reaping rich harvests from 'capturing the masses'. And the outlook for Capitol was far from bleak. In just thirteen years it had established itself as America's fourth biggest seller, with annual sales in 1955 worth more than $17 million.

E.M.I., as the biggest recording organization in the world, might reasonably have expected huge profits from the demand for American records. But the sales boom coincided with the final breakdown of its transatlantic exchange agreements with Columbia and RCA-Victor. For some time, both of these American companies had been unhappy about their contracts with E.M.I., each believing it was getting the worse of the deal, and E.M.I., beset by management problems, could not put up a convincing case as to why the agreements should continue. Although Columbia and RCA each sold more than a million records pressed from E.M.I. matrices in the United States each year, E.M.I. was selling nearly six million discs recorded by the Americans.

Columbia was the first to make the break, in 1954. It was a double blow for E.M.I. It lost all the biggest-selling American artists in the catalogue — at least half of its popular repertoire — plus an outlet for British recordings in the United States. RCA-

Jo Stafford, who recorded for Capitol, was, together with Frank Sinatra, a member of the Pied Pipers vocal back-up group for Tommy Dorsey's Orchestra.

The Andrews Sisters, Maxine, Patty and Laverne.

Dinah Shore

Les Paul and Mary Ford

Victor threatened to follow suit immediately, thus completely cutting off E.M.I.'s supply of American recording artists. That it agreed to a brief reprieve was thanks entirely to the man the E.M.I. board had called in to sort out the company's desperate problems.

Joseph Lockwood, a prominent British industrialist, had agreed to take over as chairman only after a lot of persuading and, when he arrived at E.M.I. he was appalled at what he found. Hidebound by outdated business practices, secrecy and an apparent disregard of the need to make profits, the company was very nearly bankrupt. Lockwood had to borrow £1 million during his first three months, simply to pay wages. At his first board meeting, he discovered that two directors were in the habit of playing chess under the table. The others passed the time in long-winded discussions about their musical likes and dislikes, with each director demanding to know when his favourite classical piece was going to be recorded by his favourite artists. Someone asked Lockwood what kind of music he preferred, and the new chairman took the chance to show from the start how he was going to run things. He told the board bluntly: 'The only music I care about is music that sells.'

No music was selling faster then than American pop, but E.M.I.'s share of it was in danger of disappearing. Lockwood had lost Columbia. Now he sent two executives to the United States in an attempt to postpone the split with RCA-Victor until E.M.I. had found a new outlet in America. Then he opened urgent negotiations with the chiefs of Capitol Records. Early in 1955, E.M.I. bought the company for $8,500,000. Most advisers told Lockwood that the price was too high. But he knew that the cost of not having access to the American artists and the US market was too disastrous to contemplate.

Capitol staff in Los Angeles feared an invasion of British businessmen with bowler hats and umbrellas, intent on telling them how to run their affairs. But Lockwood was far too canny to interfere with an organization which was doing perfectly well and growing steadily. The only regular contact between the two companies after the takeover was a weekly telephone call which Lockwood made early every Monday morning from his bed in London to Glenn Wallichs in California, where it was still Sunday evening. It usually lasted about forty minutes.

Despite the acquisition of Capitol, which restored Frank Sinatra to the E.M.I. catalogue, the loss of Columbia and RCA-Victor was a tremendous blow. Britain had no artists capable of stemming the tide of American-made hit records. Donald Peers, Alma Cogan, Ronnie Hilton and Eve Boswell were all turning out reasonable discs, but sales were puny compared to those of the US 'swoon-crooners'.

◄ Judy Garland, the child star who turned into another entertainment legend.

STUDIO HARCOURT

DISQUES Columbia

EDITH PIAF

Edith Piaf, 'the little sparrow'

Some consolation came from France, where a talented foursome of best-selling singers started making inroads into the British market. Three were men: Tino Rossi, the Corsican-born heart-throb who wowed the customers at the Casino de Paris, and had hits with 'Marinella' on record and *The Godfather* on the film screen; Jean Sablon, who was among the first *chanson* singers to master microphone techniques and treat recording as an art, and who had issued the last disc before the Nazi invasion in 1940, 'Le Fiacre'; and Charles Trenet, whose optimistic style gave him a world-wide hit with his own song, 'La Mer'. The fourth was a woman who has become one of the legends of popular music.

Edith Piaf, the little sparrow, was the star who, to Frenchmen, epitomized the *chanson*, bringing to its passionate balance of lyric and music all the emotion of a life that had seen more than its share of highs and lows. Deserted by her circus parents on the streets of Paris as a baby, she was blind at eight, cured miraculously at the Lisieux shrine of St Thérèse, involved in a murder investigation when a café owner who befriended her was killed, was married twice, injured in a bad car crash, and frequently ill. But she refused to let bad luck beat her, and produced a string of memorable best-sellers: 'Hymne à L'amour', 'Padam ... Padam', 'Milord' and her theme-song, 'Non, je ne regrette rien'. Maurice Chevalier and Marlene Dietrich worshipped her, Yves Montand, Guilbert Bécaud and Charles Aznavour owe their showbusiness lucky breaks to her and, when she died in October 1963, 120,000 people lined her route to the grave in a Valentino-style display of genuine mourning.

If Edith Piaf regretted nothing, E.M.I. had

Tino Rossi (above) and Charles Trenet (below) represented a different France, a France of entertainment and music-hall tradition. Trenet's own song 'La Mer' still sells today, thirty-five years on.

CHARLES TRENET
Le Fou chantant
GRAND PRIX DU DISQUE 1939

Columbia

The arrival of Elvis Presley on the music scene totally changed the record business.
Where before a few hundred thousand records represented a major hit, Presley's
records sold in such huge numbers that the entire industry had to rethink and
adjust to new dimensions, a process which led to both undreamed of prosperity
and wealth for performers and record companies alike, but also carried within it
the seeds of an eventual reckoning.

plenty of reasons to be sorry in 1956, when the full extent of what it was losing with the departure of RCA-Victor was made clear. It was one of Wally Ridley's tasks at HMV to listen to the new American offerings and decide which to release in Britain. Just before the final break, a parcel of six records arrived from RCA with a note that read: 'You won't understand anything about this, but do issue two sides because this fellow's going to be very big.' Ridley, a songwriter, manager and record producer, thought there was little he did not know about pop . . . but he was baffled as he listened to those six discs. 'I couldn't understand a goddamn word,' he recalled. 'I kept putting my ear to the box to try to understand what this fellow was singing about. In the end I got two words . . . "Heartbreak Hotel".' Elvis Presley had arrived in Europe.

To many Americans, Elvis was an abomination. One outraged churchman described him as a 'whirling dervish of sex'. No one had ever heard a white man sing that way before. No one had ever seen a singer bump and grind on stage as if, as if . . . well, one district attorney summed up the feelings of many perturbed parents by describing the act as 'obscenely suggestive'. Long sideburns, a greased ducktail hairstyle and a defiantly curled upper lip helped make Presley a symbol who, some said, would corrupt the nation's youth. Only a year before, kids had ripped cinema seats from their mountings when Bill Haley and his Comets belted out 'Rock Around The Clock' in the film *Blackboard Jungle*. Now this ex-truck-driver from Tupelo, Mississippi, threatened even more unimaginable horrors.

But nobody was worrying at RCA-Victor, the company which had signed Presley for $35,000. Astonished executives watched the line on their sales graph curl steeply upwards and shoot off the top of the paper; between August and December 1956, Presley was No. 1 in the charts every week. By the end of the year he had sold more than ten million records, and won seven gold discs for such hits as 'Heartbreak Hotel', 'Hound Dog' and 'Love Me Tender'. All over the world, Elvis and rock'n'roll unleashed a record boom far beyond anyone's wildest dreams. Sales in the United States tripled in just four years. For the first time since the war, youngsters had money in their pockets and they spent it lavishly on the discs of Presley, Pat Boone, the Everly Brothers, Paul Anka, Bobby Darin and Little Richard. Mannie Sachs, head of RCA-Victor, predicted sales of around $300 million for 1959. He was hopelessly wrong – sales rocketed to $511 million. Capitol Records shared in the boom; the company bought by E.M.I. for less than £3 million four years earlier was quoted on the New York Stock Exchange as being worth £85 million.

Every big American record company began a frantic search for a rock'n'roll singer it could promote as its own 'Elvis'. None of them had much enthusiasm for rock music. Without exception, they preferred the safer, more melodious songs of 'real' singers such as Crosby and Sinatra. But rock was clearly the big moneymaker. Columbia found a 'new Presley' with the apt name of Johnny Cash. MGM signed a Mississippi-born rockabilly singer called Harold Jenkins, and re-christened him Conway Twitty. Decca discovered the legendary Buddy Holly in a Nashville talent show. And Capital A&R man Ken Nelson found an ex-merchant-seaman from Norfolk, Virginia, who looked uncannily like Elvis, and sang a little like him, too.

Gene Vincent left the navy after a motorcycle accident in 1955, and began singing with a country-&-western band on a local radio station. A friendly DJ persuaded them to make a demonstration tape and send it to Capitol. It arrived at precisely the right moment in the great Presley hunt. Capitol flew Vincent and his group, the Bluecaps, to Nashville, and re-recorded the song on their tape, 'Be-Bop-A-Lula'. The session was not without its problems. The Bluecaps' lead guitarist was unable to play at anything less than full volume, and in the end Vincent had to be put in another room so that his voice could be heard; engineers used a 'flutter echo' to beef up his high-pitched voice; the result was a million-

Gene Vincent

The recording career of Gene Vincent was cut short when he died of bleeding ulcers in 1971. His tough and aggressive 'rock 'n' roll rebel' image was quite the reverse off stage. He never received Top Ten status, but the memory of this cult figure keeps the songs 'Be-Bop-A-Lula', 'Blue Gene Bop' and 'Wild Cat' right at the top.

244

selling hit. But Vincent made only one more big-selling record, 'Lotta Lovin' ', before his career dropped into the doldrums. He overdid the greasy, vicious image of rock'n'roll. His all-leather stage gear, and brash, tasteless lyrics – 'I'm lookin' for a woman with a one-track mind, a-fuggin' and a-kissin' and a-smoochin' all the time' – were nearly two decades ahead of their time, and alienated both the critics and the kids who bought records. In 1960, while touring Britain with his friend Eddie Cochran, he was injured in another road crash. Cochran, then high in the charts with 'Three Steps To Heaven', was killed.

Capitol's quest for a rock'n'roll winner went on. Esquerita, its answer to Little Richard, cut a series of bizarre rock tracks with a group of musicians determined to take off in their own searing solos, regardless of what the rest of the band was doing. One critic wrote: 'If a producer or arranger was deputed to the sessions, he must have been bound and gagged and put in a corner.' In singer Tommy Sands, country-boogie pianist Merril Moore and Johnny Otis, the 'godfather of rhythm and blues', Capitol had more promising artists, but their material was generally poor, a cheap caricature of the real thing, and the label's reputation among rock fans suffered.

In other fields, Capitol had better luck. Country singer Sonny James sold a million copies of 'Young Love', despite the competition from a cover version by Tab Hunter, and the Kingston Trio's 'Tom Dooley' – the first pop 'death disc' – was a monster hit, helped by unwitting publicity generated by clergymen and parent-teacher groups who attacked its 'corrupt and depraved' lyrics. Capitol also cashed in on film soundtracks. The album of *Oklahoma!*, with Gordon MacRae, Shirley Jones and Gene Nelson, is still regarded as one of the all-time-great records. Another best-seller was the music from *The King And I*, while Bing Crosby, Frank Sinatra and Louis Armstrong shared the honours on *High Society*, perhaps the most successful original film score on record, with such hits as 'True Love', 'Now You Has Jazz', and the unforgettable Crosby–Sinatra classic, 'Well, Did You Ever'.

The tragic, brilliant Judy Garland signed for Capitol in the late '50s. Suicide attempts, repeated breakdowns and a growing reliance on drugs had all threatened to end her career. But on 23 April 1961, before a distinguished audience at New York's Carnegie Hall, Judy staged a courageous comeback that re-established her as one of America's greatest entertainers. The audience willed her to be wonderful, and she was. It was the exciting performance of a lifetime, captured by Capitol on a double album, *Judy At The Carnegie Hall*. Amid the wild applause at the end, a tearful, exultant voice can just be heard, saying simply: 'Thank you, I love you very much.'

Early in the '60s, Capitol's rock fortunes received a boost from a totally unexpected direction: the beaches of California. Thousands of kids spent their weekends and vacations riding the Pacific rollers on surfboards. In 1961, five of them – three brothers, a cousin and a neighbour – got together in the respectable middle-class Los Angeles suburb of Hawthorne to form a close-harmony group and sing surfing anthems. A music publisher who heard them was impressed enough to offer them the chance to record on a small local label. The

Cliff Richard appeared to be the answer to the British search for a native talent to compete with America's Presley. He wasn't, but the singer has grown remarkably in stature and talent and still is a major recording star today, having outlasted Elvis, the Beatles and many others in between.

boys had no drums, so percussion was provided by banging a dustbin. But their sound caught on, and sales swelled as youngsters passed on news of the disc when they met on the beach. The group, who called themselves the Pendletons after the make of shirt favoured by surfers, began appearing at clubs and local dances. They changed their billing to Carl and the Passions but soon tired of that name, too. Finally they settled on the Beach Boys.

When a Capitol producer heard a tape of their sound, he immediately offered a contract. And within months the Beach Boys were making waves in the national charts with 'Surfin' Safari', then 'Surfin' USA', then 'Surfer Girl'. Their melodic soft-rock tunes and lyrics reflected part of the·American dream: golden beaches, curling waves, sun-tanned blond kids, endless leisure. A string of imitators soon climbed on to the surfboard, chasing another part of the American dream – big money.

In Britain, pop-music producers were starting to find their own money-spinning stars. Joseph Lockwood had freed the E.M.I. company from the constraints of a board which, for too long, had looked on popular repertoire as a necessary evil to keep the vulgar masses amused. 'Before I arrived,' the chairman recalled, 'the classical producers were the field marshals of the company and the pop producers were treated like lance-corporals. I changed that straight away, brought the pop people out and told them that, from the business point of view, they were more important than the classical department.' E.M.I.'s quartet of pop producers, Norman Newell and Wally Ridley on the HMV label, Norrie Paramor at Columbia and George Martin at Parlophone, were amply to justify Lockwood's faith over the next few years as they scoured the country looking for 'music that sells'.

Paramor discovered a seventeen-year-old boy called Harry Webb playing in London coffee bars. He had formed his own rock'n'roll group after seeing a Bill Haley concert. Paramor changed the lad's name to Cliff Richard, and within a year he was in the charts with 'Move It', the first of nearly eighty hits over the next twenty-three years. Around the same time, an Irish girl called Ruby Murray, a Columbia protégée, had five records in the Top Twenty simultaneously – a feat no British artist has equalled since. HMV also signed Malcolm Vaughan after getting a tip-off about an exciting new singer appearing at the Chiswick Empire. When producer Ridley found at their first recording session that he had absolutely no sense of musical time, Ridley stood at the other side of the microphone, mouthing the words of 'St Theresa Of The Roses' so that Vaughan did not miss the beat. The single was a smash hit.

Overnight sensations were the rule rather than the exception by 1960. First, Terry Nelhams from Acton changed his name to Adam Faith and soared up the charts with 'What Do You Want?' then a fourteen-year-old schoolgirl called Helen Shapiro caused an even bigger stir by taking both 'You Don't Know' and 'Walking Back To Happiness' to No. 1. They were heady, exciting, volatile days. Pop music was constantly making headlines, and no one really knew which records would be hits, or why. Frank Ifield, an Australian singer

The Beach Boys

This illustrious group on the Capitol Records label surely must be one of America's greatest contributors of contemporary music during the '60s. The harmony construction for their songs 'Good Vibrations', 'God Only Knows' and, earlier, 'I Get Around' and 'Sloop John B' was unsurpassed. The pen of group member Brian Wilson gave them a wave of twenty-three hit records throughout the world.

on an eight-record contract with Columbia, asked if he could yodel on the last of them. Columbia agreed – they planned to drop him anyway, as his previous records had all flopped. 'I Remember You' was released without any promotion, but after only one airing on Radio Luxembourg, it became one of the fastest-selling singles ever. Demand was so great that the E.M.I. factory at Hayes could not cope, and rivals Decca agreed to help out by pressing copies. Ifield rocketed to the top of the charts and, instead of being dropped by Columbia, became one of the label's hottest properties, if only briefly.

American pop stars still sold well in Britain, but the transatlantic traffic was all one way. Britain's new breed of singers failed to set female hearts aflutter across the Atlantic, the way they did in Europe. Cliff Richard's first million-selling disc, 'Living Doll', was No. 1 in Britain for six weeks in 1960, but never got higher than No. 30 in the United States, and his tour there that year flopped disastrously. But Americans who thought they could afford to ignore the best that Britain had to offer indefinitely were in for a rude awakening. George Martin had kept his Parlophone label ticking over nicely by making successful comedy records with stars such as Peter Ustinov, Spike Milligan and Peter Sellers. Parlophone was the E.M.I. baby, smaller than either HMV or Columbia, and its musical artists had nothing like the same stature as those of the two bigger labels. Then, one day in the summer of 1962, Martin received a telephone call from a friend who worked at the HMV shop in London's Oxford Street. A group of four northern lads had come in to make a 'demo disc', he was told. They had rough accents and used a weird name, but it might be worth his time to listen to them. These four lads were to spearhead a new revolution in pop, and add the strangest name yet to the music machine's hall of fame . . . the name of the Beatles.

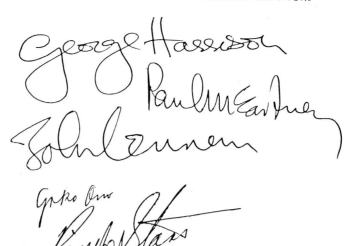

DATE	NAME	OF/OR REPRESENTING
JUNE 5th 1968	MR. GEORGE HARRISON MR. JOHN LENNON MR PAUL McCARTNEY MR. RINGO STARR	} 'THE BEATLES'
	YOKO ONO (female)	

BEATLEMANIA

On 28 October 1961, a young man called Raymond Jones walked into a record shop in Liverpool – and lit the fuse for the most amazing pop-music success story of all time. He asked for a disc called 'My Bonnie'. The man behind the counter, Brian Epstein, had never heard of it. But the twenty-seven-year-old businessman prided himself on meeting the needs of customers at his family-owned store. That evening he went to a dingy club called the Cavern to listen to the group Jones had mentioned. He was impressed by the female adulation that greeted the lively, raucous beat of the four players, who called themselves the Beatles. He ordered two hundred copies of 'My Bonnie', the record they had made backing a singer called Tony Sheridan. And on 13 December 1961, he became the group's manager. It was the first step in a fairy tale that was to make all five millionaires – and revitalize popular music.

The rock 'n' roll revolution, launched on a wave of teenage hysteria in 1955, had run out of steam by 1962. The exciting unpredictability of early Haley and Presley songs had been lost in a welter of carbon-copy covers as the recording industry got a grip on the new market created by a generation of affluent teenagers. The raw sounds had been orchestrated and exploited into a smoothly controlled, commercially acceptable product. British pop stars arrived pre-packaged as if from a production line: Marty Wilde, Billy Fury, Eden Kane, Craig Douglas, Jess Conrad, all fresh-faced nice guys covering American songs and styles.

America and Elvis still led the way up the charts. Sam Cooke and Chubby Checker introduced the Twist, Little Eva launched the Locomotion. The Crystals and Ronettes cashed in on boy-meets-girl spectaculars orchestrated by Phil Spector, and Mary Wells, Marvin Gaye and the Miracles gave Berry Gordy's Tamla-Motown stable its first hits. Popular music seemed to have settled into a competent, complacent, respectable, reasonably profitable groove.

◄The Beatles' first entry into the EMI visitors book. Someone there had to explain who the lads were. With George Martin their producer.

The Beatles' first venue, 'The Cavern' in Liverpool

But in the clubs and pubs of the industrial North, of Birmingham and of London, hundreds of groups were playing a different kind of music: hard-hitting, gutsy, essentially simple rock that owed a lot to the influence of Chuck Berry, Little Richard, and rhythm and blues singers few British pop fans had ever heard of. The Beatles were among the best of them. John Lennon, Paul McCartney, George Harrison and drummer Pete Best had a huge following on Merseyside, and had also worked the clubs of Hamburg's seedier side, a harsh training-ground which helped them develop the attack and vitality of their style. Their songs had a harder, more down-to-earth edge than the teenage love ballads dominating the charts. And that proved a problem when Brian Epstein brought them south to London, looking for a recording contract. At first no one wanted to know: Pye, Philips, HMV and Columbia were all unimpressed. Decca A&R man Dick Rowe said groups with guitars were 'on the way out' and advised Epstein to stick to selling records in Liverpool. In desperation, Epstein took his protégés to the HMV record shop in Oxford Street, hoping a properly made 'demo disc' would make the companies think again. Then he was directed to George Martin.

At that time the Parlophone chief was looking for a singer who could provide him with the kind of success Cliff Richard was having with the Shadows on Columbia. And while the Beatles ran through their limited repertoire at the audition on 6 June 1962, Martin eyed each of them individually through the control-room window, trying to decide which could be turned into a lead singer. Paul had the sweeter voice, but John was the more forceful personality. In the end, he decided to leave them as they were. 'Frankly, their material didn't impress me, least of all their own songs,' Martin admitted later. 'I felt I was going to have to provide suitable material for them, and was quite certain that their songwriting ability had no saleable future. But the group as a whole confirmed by their playing my earlier feeling that we might be able to do something together.'

In July, Martin offered them a tentative contract; the terms were hardly generous: Parlophone would guarantee to issue a minimum of four titles, and pay a royalty of one (old) penny per record. This would increase by one farthing (a coin already out of circulation) for each of four subsequent years. Epstein swallowed hard and signed. He knew a recording contract on any terms was better than nothing. There was one other condition: Pete Best had to go. Epstein recruited Ringo Starr, a drummer with another Liverpool group, and on 11 September the Beatles returned to Abbey Road to make their first record.

Martin had intended to provide the songs, but at the last moment he relented, and let the lads record two Lennon–McCartney numbers, 'Love Me Do' and 'PS I Love You'. It was a long, tough session. The Beatles ran through 'Love Me Do' fifteen times before Martin was satisfied. By then John Lennon's lips were numb from playing the harmonica riff over and over again. The record was released without ceremony on 4 October.

Martin was not surprised when E.M.I. decided not to spend money promoting it. When he had announced at the regular monthly meeting of all E.M.I. label producers that

The Ed Sullivan Show in 1964, which cemented the Fab Four's supremacy. Ed Sullivan and Brian Epstein on the left.

he planned to release a record by a group called the Beatles, his colleagues had fallen about laughing. Some thought it must be another Parlophone comedy disc. One suggested it was Spike Milligan in disguise. 'I'm serious,' Martin told them. 'This is a great group and we're going to hear a lot more from them.' The record was not even thought worth plugging on the programme E.M.I. sponsored on commercial Radio Luxembourg and the Beatles were unable to promote it personally, because they had another booking in Hamburg. Yet 'Love Me Do' crept, unheralded, to No. 17 in the charts, helped by the 10,000 copies Epstein had ordered for his Liverpool shop.

The police had their hands full wherever the Beatles showed up.

In November, the Beatles were back at Abbey Road to record a follow-up. Martin wanted them to use a Mitch Murray song called 'How Do You Do It?'. The group didn't like it, and argued for their own song, 'Please Please Me'. Eventually Martin allowed them to record both. After only one take of 'Please Please Me', he pressed the intercom button in the control room and said: 'Gentlemen, you have just made your first No. 1 record.'

He was right. 'Please Please Me' was released in January to an enthusiastic welcome from critics. One said the Beatles had 'every chance of becoming the big star attraction of 1963'. In the same week, the group appeared on nationwide television for the first time, in a

Cilla Black

pop show called *Thank Your Lucky Stars*. Their curious mop-top haircuts and collarless jackets made as big an impression as the music. On 2 March, 'Please Please Me' reached No. 1 in the charts. George Martin hastily recorded an LP in a marathon thirteen-hour session at Abbey Road. It too went to No. 1, and stayed in the album charts for six months. And a collection of four songs from it became the first EP ever to top the singles Top Twenty.

Dazzled by his initial success, Brian Epstein began looking for other acts in the clubs and dance-halls of Liverpool. He signed Gerry and the Pacemakers, who had been playing on Merseyside for four years, and George Martin recorded them singing the number the Beatles rejected, 'How Do You Do it?'. On 22 March they were at No. 1. A few weeks later, Epstein arrived at Abbey Road with Billy J. Kramer, after buying him from his previous manager for £50. Martin said his voice was not good enough for recording, but Epstein was persistent. So Martin recorded him singing Lennon and McCartney's 'Do You Want To Know A Secret?', then double-tracked the voice to try to cover its weakness, and added a loud piano accompaniment. To his amazement, that single too soared to No. 1. 'The process was starting to seem almost inevitable,' Martin recalled.

Next, Epstein came south with Priscilla White, the cloakroom girl at Liverpool's Cavern Club. He changed her name to Cilla Black and again overcame Martin's reservations – Martin called her 'a rock and roll screecher with a piercing nasal sound'. Her first record, a Lennon—McCartney song called 'Love Of The Loved', disappeared almost without trace. But the next, a Burt Bacharach song called 'Anyone Who Had A Heart', followed the Parlophone pattern by zooming to No. 1.

Rival record producers trekked north to Lancashire, desperate now to find a group to rival the one they had all rejected. But it was George Martin's assistant, Ron Richards, who found the new sensation. He signed a five-man Manchester group called the Hollies, and soon they too were reeling off the hits, with 'I'm Alive', 'Carrie-Anne' and 'On A Carousel'. The Beatles had opened the door for almost any group with guitars and drums and, for a while, stardom was just one hit-record away. From Tyneside came the Animals, with Alan Price's organ adding refinement behind Eric Burdon's gravelly vocals on big-sellers like 'House Of The Rising Sun'. From Birmingham came the Spencer Davis Group, nurturing Stevie Winwood, later to form Traffic. From Lancashire came the Searchers, the Swinging Blue Jeans, and Freddie and the Dreamers. And from the thriving London R&B scene came Manfred Mann, Eric Clapton and the Yardbirds, and the Rolling Stones. Epstein had steered the Beatles away from a head-on clash with what was socially acceptable. They may have been long-haired, brash and witty, but they were polite and wore suits. The Stones, on the other hand, were the nonconformist brats of rock and roll, an image carefully fostered by their shrewd manager, Andrew Loog Oldham.

None of the other groups, however, could compete with the newly christened Fab Four. The Beatles toured Britain to scenes of increasing hysteria. Screaming girls drowned the music as they rattled off their growing list of hits, then made a hurried getaway by car

◄ The only female artist of the Beatle era, managed then by Brian Epstein. She not only survived the avalanche of Liverpool groups in the '60s by achieveing eleven Top Ten singles, but went on with her successful career that now spans two decades.

The Yardbirds.

Dave Clark Five.

Billy J. Kramer.

Manfred Mann.

The Hollies

◄ The Yardbirds

This group was the formidable beginnings for three of the greatest rock guitarists of the recent past – Jimmy Page, Eric Clapton and Jeff Beck. Other notable members included the record producer Paul Sanwell Smith, Jim McCarty and the late Keith Relf.

Dave Clark Five

These five very popular boys came from Tottenham in London and achieved one of the biggest selling singles, in the history of EMI, on both sides of the Atlantic aptly called 'Glad All Over'. They entered the UK charts on twenty-two occasions between 1963 and 1970.

Billy J. Kramer (and the Dakotas)

One of Liverpool's young idols of the Sixties whose short chart success gave him a string of hits from 1963–1965 with two No. 1 records 'Bad to Me' and 'Little Children' In-house EMI producer, George Martin was at the helm.

Manfred Mann

This innovative group, fronted by Manfred himself, with originally Paul Jones as lead singer, later replaed, by Mike D'Abo, enjoyed six Top Ten singles with HMV. Notably 'Pretty Flamingo'.

The Hollies

The only British band to outstrip the Beatles number of chart entries of 26 with the massive score of twenty-seven hit. Twenty-four were recorded for Parlophone, of which eleven, were Top Five, the biggest 'I'm Alive' went to number No. 1 in May 1965.

through hordes of fans besieging the theatres and concert-halls. In October 1963, they returned from a trip to Sweden to a rapturous welcome from thousands of shrieking teenagers at Heathrow Airport. On 13 October they topped the bill on the country's top TV show, *Sunday Night At The London Palladium*. Tens of thousands of locked-out fans packed the streets around the theatre, and next morning the *Daily Mirror* newspaper headlined its account of the amazing scenes with a word which was to be used again and again over the next few months – Beatlemania. Even the Royal Family caught the fever. In November, the group appeared in the Royal Variety Command Performance show. John Lennon brought the house down by saying: 'On the next number, would those in the cheap seats clap their hands . . . and the rest of you rattle your jewellery.'

As 'She Loves You' followed 'From Me To You' to the top of the charts, Brian Epstein was kept busy negotiating franchise deals for Beatle T-shirts, Beatle magazines, Beatle jackets, Beatle boots, Beatle posters, Beatle dolls. As Ringo Starr said: 'Every time you spell beetle with an A, we get some money.' Boys were sent home from school for sporting Beatle haircuts, rioting girls were hosed down in Plymouth, and a vicar suggested a Beatle-style

Artist Peter Blake assembled the *Sergeant Pepper* cover. Notes include Jesus and Hitler which were later dropped as being incompatible.

LENNY BRUCE
STAN LAUREL
FRED ASTAIRE
JUNG
JHONNY WEISMULLER
ROBERT PEEL
H G WELLS
ALISTAIR CROWLEY (HEAD)

STUART SUTCLIFFE
BEARDSLEY
JESUS?
INDIAN HEAD (WHITE BEARD)

DYLAN THOMAS
TYRONE POWER
STEPHEN CRANE,
ALDOUS HUXLEY.
ISSY BONN

17

JAMES JOYCE   MAE WEST
OSCAR WILDE   CROWLEY 2
ADOLF HITLER   INDIAN HEAD
RICHARD MERTIN,   BURTON ETC
MARLENE DEITRICH   W.C. FIELDS
LEO GORCEY   LEWIS CARROLL
HUNTZ HALL   R LIDNER
BOBBY BREEN   E A. POE 2.

EDGAR ALLAN POE
SHIRLEY TEMPLE   28
SNOW WHITE
DORATHEA
         LANGE,
   COCTEAU.
 BETTE DAVIS
 PETTY GIRLS
  EINSTEIN,
 KARL MARX
  GANDHI,
   INDIAN.
    INDIAN

1989
SEN

Christmas carol on the lines of, 'O Come All Ye Faithful, Yeah Yeah Yeah'.

The group's second album, *With The Beatles*, was released in November 1963 with advance orders of 250,000 copies. And their fifth single, 'I Want To Hold Your Hand', went straight to No. 1 on the strength of an incredible one million advance orders. At the end of the year, a stunned George Martin realized that his previously obscure record label had topped the charts for thirty-seven of the fifty-two weeks in 1963. And the British sound had totally obliterated the American stars. Only Elvis Presley had made it to No. 1, with 'Devil In Disguise' – and that stayed there for only one week.

The following year, the Beatles turned the tide even further – by invading America. E.M.I.'s American outlet, Capitol Records, had been unmoved by the Beatles' early successes in Britain. When George Martin sent a copy of 'Please Please Me' to Capitol president Alan Livingston, he received the curt reply: 'We don't think the Beatles will do anything in this market.' Martin tried in vain to interest him in subsequent singles, and only after pressure from E.M.I. management in London did Capitol at last agree reluctantly to issue one record, 'to see how it goes'. It went. 'I Want To Hold Your Hand' was released in America on 13 January 1964 and became the fastest-selling Capitol single ever. One million copies were snapped up in three weeks, and by 1 February it was topping the Billboard chart. Six days later, the group were on a plane heading west. A New York radio station announced: 'It is now 6.30 a.m. Beatle time, they left London thirty minutes ago. They're out over the Atlantic Ocean heading for New York. The temperature is thirty-two Beatle degrees . . .'

When they touched down at Kennedy Airport, 10,000 fans lined the roofs of every nearby building to sing, 'We love you, Beatles, oh yes we do.' When they appeared on the coast-to-coast Ed Sullivan TV show, more than 50,000 people applied for the 728 studio seats, and 73 million viewers tuned in. It was later claimed that no teenager committed a crime anywhere in the United States while the programme was screened. Within days, middle-aged men anxious to portray youthful vitality were spotted striding down New York's Park Avenue wearing Beatle wigs. By the first week in April, the Beatles held the top five places in the Billboard chart, with 'Can't Buy Me Love', 'Twist And Shout', 'She Loves You', 'I Want To Hold Your Hand' and 'Please Please Me'. Beatle records were also at Nos. 16, 44, 49, 69, 78, 84 and 88. Soon the group accounted for fifty per cent of Capitol's total sales.

The astonishing success in America was mirrored back home. In June 1964 came the première of the first Beatles film, *Hard Day's Night*, which purported to show something of what their lives had become: imprisonment by fame. In December they occupied seven slots in the British Top Twenty, and comedienne Dora Bryan was also in the chart with her novelty disc, 'All I Want For Christmas Is A Beatle'. Lennon and McCartney were also writing hits for others. Peter and Gordon went to No. 1 with 'World Without Love'; Billy J. Kramer scored with 'Bad To Me' and 'I'll Keep You Satisfied'; Cilla Black sold well with

'It's For You' and 'Step Inside Love'; and even the Rolling Stones climbed on the band-wagon of their so-called rivals, recording 'I Wanna Be Your Man'.

At Abbey Road, away from the frenzy of the fans, a working relationship of great mutual respect had grown between George Martin and the Beatles. At the beginning, Martin later recalled, he would sit and listen to what they had written, then suggest the changes demanded for a successful record. 'All I wanted from them was good songs, and those they gave me,' he said. 'At the start I thought, "God, this can't last for ever." But they amazed me with their fertility. To begin with the material was fairly crude, but they developed their writing ability very quickly; the harmonies, the songs themselves, became cleverer. As the style emerged and the recording techniques developed, so my control over what the finished product sounded like increased. Yet at the same time, my need for changing the pure music became less and less. As I could see their talent growing, I could recognize that an idea coming from them was better than an idea coming from me. In a sense I made a tactical withdrawal, recognizing that theirs was the greater talent.'

One after another, Beatles singles went straight to No. 1 immediately they were issued. 'Can't Buy Me Love' had the biggest advance sales of any record ever released: a million in Britain, more than two million in America. It topped the charts in every record-buying country in the world. 'Ticket To Ride', 'Help!', the theme from their second film, 'Day Tripper', 'Paperback Writer' all followed. No artists had ever dominated the market to such an incredible extent.

Not everyone thought that was a good thing. In Britain, Paul Johnson droned in the *New Statesman*: 'Those who flock round the Beatles, who scream themselves into hysteria, whose vacant faces flicker over the TV screens, are the least fortunate of their generation, the dull, the idle, the failures.' In America, evangelist Billy Graham dismissed the Beatles as 'a passing phase, symptoms of the uncertainty of the times and the confusion about us'. But both were voices in the wilderness. And Johnson could not have been more wrong. If Presley and the early rockers had brought black-style music to the working-class whites, the Beatles were refining it into a style that captivated the middle classes and even the Establishment. The *Help!* album produced the hauntingly beautiful song, 'Yesterday'. And on *Revolver* came 'Eleanor Rigby', the number which, according to writer Denis Norden, forced the boundaries of popular music to be redrawn. The *Sunday Times* hailed Lennon and McCartney as the 'greatest composers since Beethoven'.

In June 1967 came the album many still regard as the most influential in the history of pop music, *Sergeant Pepper's Lonely Hearts Club Band*. It was originally Paul's song, and his idea to make the LP as if the band really existed, even dubbing in applause at certain points to give the illusion of a live stage-show. The three other Beatles accepted the plan with enthusiasm, and from that moment, according to George Martin, it was as if *Pepper* had 'a life of its own'.

A total of seven hundred hours' recording time and £40,000 went into the making of the album over nine months. Day after day, and long into the night, George Martin toiled away in the Abbey Road studios with John, Paul, George and Ringo. Innovation and improvisation abounded as a multiplicity of styles and subjects were woven into an integrated suite. The Beatles led mainstream pop into the underground worlds of drug-culture psychedelia and fantasy, and matched the startling new approach to songs with advanced production techniques, creating the first eight-track recording by linking two four-track tape machines. George Martin filled in the gaps by capturing the myriad special effects the Beatles demanded. Lennon wanted circus music to 'swirl up and around' at the end of 'Being For The Benefit Of Mr Kite'. So Martin cut tapes of Victorian steam-organ music into twelve-inch lengths, scattered them over the floor, then stuck them together in random order. Mixed with organ and harmonica tracks, they became a background 'wash' of Big-Top sound.

As a twenty-four bar finale to 'A Day In The Life', the album's last track, the Beatles asked for a tremendous build-up of sound, 'from nothing to something like the end of the world'. Martin hired half a symphony orchestra and, at Paul's behest, the forty-two musicians arrived in full evening dress. Martin told them the lowest and highest notes he needed, and added that it was every man for himself in between them. The musicians fell in with the spirit of the recording. As they taped the chaotic crescendo, the Beatles and their friends passed among them, handing out sparklers, joints and funny hats. One distinguished violinist wore a bright red false nose and paper spectacles while he played. Another held his bow in a giant gorilla claw.

When *Sergeant Pepper* was at last finished, the Beatles turned their attention to the sleeve. They had commissioned pop artist Peter Blake to amass a sea of faces of their heroes, dead and alive. They included everyone from Karl Marx to Shirley Temple, from W.C. Fields to Gandhi, from Laurel and Hardy to Bob Dylan. E.M.I. officials took one look and refused to allow the sleeve to be printed. They feared an avalanche of writs from outraged celebrities. The Beatles appealed direct to chairman Lockwood, by now Sir Joseph. Two of the country's most eminent lawyers, Lord Goodman and Lord Shawcross, had told him the design was 'dynamite', and he did his best to get the Fab Four to drop the idea. But they were adamant. Lockwood finally agreed to sanction the cover, as long as the Beatles indemnified E.M.I. to the tune of £10 million, and obtained the permission of everyone in their collage who was still alive.

Paul McCartney could not see what all the fuss was about. He was sure most people would be pleased to be seen on a Beatles album. 'Don't you believe it,' a glum Sir Joseph told him. 'We'll get hundreds of lawsuits.' But Paul was right. The boys cabled conductor Leonard Bernstein in New York to ask his permission. Back came the telegram: 'Delighted.' In the end, the only face removed was Gandhi's. 'We contacted about a third of the people involved before we gave up,' Sir Joseph recalled. 'The cover was released with comparatively few permissions, but we never had a single letter of complaint from anyone. I couldn't believe it.' (The fuss about the faces blinded the E.M.I. board to something else in the picture that they would have objected to: the potted palms around the big drum were thriving marijuana plants.)

Radio stations were given the go-ahead to start playing *Sergeant Pepper* a week before its June release-date. The exact moment chosen was midnight on a Sunday in America, the time most stations shut down to service their transmitters. That Sunday in June, none of

them went off the air; instead, they played the record all through the night and all through the next day. One ecstatic American reviewer later wrote: 'The closest Western civilization has come to unity since the Congress of Vienna in 1815 was the week the *Sergeant Pepper* album was released. In every city in Europe and America, the stereo systems and radios played it. At the time I happened to be driving across country on Interstate 80. In each city where I stopped for gas or food – Laramie, Ogallala, Moline, South Bend – the melodies wafted in from some far-off radio. It was the most amazing thing I have ever heard. For a brief while the irreparably fragmented consciousness of the West was unified, at least in the minds of the young.'

Such hyperbole was typical of the media's Beatlemania. Hysteria over live appearances by the group was a thing of the past, because the Beatles had given up live appearances. Their last British concert was at Wembley in May 1966, their last American gig at San Francisco three months later. But the Press took over the excesses. A British Sunday newspaper played *Sergeant Pepper* to an audience of dogs after reporting that the final sound on the record was a note of 20,000 hertz, audible only to canine ears and liable to make hounds howl. They were disappointed. Later, newspapers all over the world whipped up a rumour that Paul McCartney had died and been replaced by a lookalike. The story was given credence on the basis of 'evidence' from the *Abbey Road* LP sleeve, on which Paul was the only Beatle crossing the road bare-footed! In a way, the Beatles had opened the door for such wild speculation by 'burying' themselves on the *Sergeant Pepper* cover. While they were photographed in brightly coloured band garb, each adopting an individual appearance, four waxworks of themselves in the old mop-tops and uniform suits stood staring blankly down at a grave bedecked with red flowers spelling out 'The Beatles'.

Within three years, fact was to catch up with fiction. On 27 August 1967, Brian Epstein was found dead at his London home. The Beatles were at Bangor, North Wales, meditating with the Maharishi Mahesh Yogi when they heard the news. At once they left for the capital. They had buried the image Epstein had given them, the image that had conquered the world; now they buried the man whose contribution to their success was greater than most people realized. His value was summed up by John Lennon when he said: 'After Brian died, we collapsed. Paul took over and supposedly led us, but we were going round in circles. We broke up then. That was the disintegration.'

The group set up their own recording and marketing organization, Apple, to try to give other artists a better start than they had had – they unearthed talented American solo singer James Taylor – but, without the guiding hand of Epstein, it soon turned into a financial nightmare. Beatle records continued to be the major source of income, but after the *Sergeant Pepper* triumph, they showed all too clearly that the greatest group the musical world had ever seen was becoming a collection of individuals, each with his own musical ideas. On the double white album of 1968, it sounded as if the rest of the group were merely session men helping out on John, Paul or George's songs.

Lennon and McCartney in particular were going in separate directions. John had left his wife Cynthia and met Japanese artist Yoko Ono. He was re-examining his ideas and values about both life and music, and heading down a path towards love, peace and eventual seclusion in New York. Paul had split with long-time girlfriend Jane Asher and met Linda Eastman, the daughter of a hard-headed New York business family. He still valued music, and was setting out on the long and winding road that would lead to more melodic hits with Wings. He was also having heated rows with George Harrison, who accused Paul of underrating his abilities as a songwriter. All four Beatles went to India to see the Maharishi, but it was George who found the deepest meaning from the mysticism. Ringo stayed only a few days before jetting back to western reality.

The simmering bad feeling erupted into the open on 11 April 1970, when Paul announced that he was quitting the group. Their musical achievements together were shoved aside by the practicalities of the great Apple débâcle. The other three Beatles called in American businessman Allen Klein to sort out the mess, but Paul did not want him, arguing the case for Linda's family to step in. The partnership was dissolved in court in 1971, but the wrangling lasted until 1977, when an out-of-court settlement of £3 million finally brought down the curtain on the Beatles.

The Beatles' feuding finale left its mark on each of them as they began their solo careers. In the break-up years, John Lennon and Yoko Ono had amazed the world by holding a lie-in for peace in Amsterdam and a press conference from inside a bag in Vienna. Some thought they were mad; more generous souls put the eccentric behaviour down to John's freedom from the constraints of group stardom. He said: 'Being a Beatle, living in that incredible fish tank, matured us in some ways but not in others. We used to meet heads of state, but we never got to see reality.' Lennon re-examined life as a Beatle in his later solo albums. Particularly poignant was his attack on his former song-writing partner Paul, called 'How Do You Sleep At Night?' George Harrison produced a superb triple album, *All Things Must Pass*, and appeared on the cover surrounded by four plastic garden gnomes. Later he produced a song that began, 'You sue me and I'll sue you . . .', an ironic commentary on the Beatle break-up. Ringo Starr's single, 'It Don't Come Easy', also had Beatle overtones.

John Lennon once said: 'None of us could have made it alone. Paul wasn't quite strong enough, I didn't have enough girl appeal, George was too quiet and Ringo was the drummer. But we thought everyone would be able to dig at least one of us, and that's how it turned out.' That, of course, was masterly understatement. There had never been anything like the Beatles. Every one of their records, singles and albums, sold more than a million copies worldwide. More than thirty sold a million in the USA alone – 'I Want To Hold Your Hand' logged up three million – and six singles sold a million in Britain. In January 1969, Hunter Davies, in his authorized biography, estimated total world sales at 260 million, counting an EP as two records and an LP as five. Since 1970, Beatle records have continued to sell in huge numbers and re-issued and re-packaged. In 1976, EMI re-released twenty-three Beatles singles, and every one made the charts again. Their songs have also made the Top Twenty when recorded by other artists – 'Yesterday' had already been covered by 119 people in 1969, and eighty other singers had recorded 'Michelle'.

But statistics alone could never capture what the Beatles meant for pop music and for their legions of fans. That was best summed up in the wave of emotion that followed the tragic shooting of John Lennon in New York in December 1980. Lennon had outraged the Establishment during the Beatle days by saying that the group were more popular than Christ. Now news of his death recalled in its dimensions the shock that swept the world when President John F. Kennedy had been gunned down in Dallas in 1963. In one brutal split-second, the dream that millions had clung to – a reunion of the Beatles – had been wiped out. It was truly the end of an era.

Marc Bolan with his band T Rex burst upon the British pop music scene in the late '60s, the first glam rock star.

HAIL… AND FAREWELL?

After the Beatles, nothing was . . . or could be . . . the same again. The sociological, musical and financial reverberations of their achievements helped to change completely the lives and attitudes of young people, pop musicians and the recorded-music industry. The Beatles had prepared the way for the most profitable age the music machine had ever seen. Ironically, the pursuit of those profits was to bring parts of the industry to its knees and sow the seeds of what could be the end of the gramophone as we know it.

Thanks largely to the Beatles, pop music in the late '60s and '70s exerted an influence it had never had before. A greater interest in it, even a commitment to certain styles and performers, became a prerequisite of acceptance by fellow teenagers.

Pop was no longer just pleasant, catchy tunes to whistle or dance to, it was taken seriously, a fundamental and often dominating part of everyday life for the most affluent young people the world had ever seen. Music was discussed, analysed, criticized, publicized and hyped in newspapers and magazines devoted to nothing else. Music flooded radio airwaves day and night, and attracted huge viewing audiences at television peak times. Music was played at home, loud and long, on expensive and sophisticated hi-fi stereos, as well as on inexpensive record players with a quality of reproduction Emile Berliner would never have believed possible.

For the musicians, too, the Beatles had created a brave new world. It was no longer essential to conform to a narrow image or style dictated by recording industry moguls. Increasingly, the company bosses had had to accept Sir Joseph Lockwood's dictum: the only music worth caring about is music that sells. There had never been such a broad spectrum of groups and solo artists exploring new sounds and subjects, defying all attempts to classify or control them. And the market was big enough for them all to find buyers.

269

Another British group, Led Zeppelin introduced ear-splitting sound levels, dubbed 'heavy metal'. Here Jimmy Page, the lead guitarist and innovative instrumentalist in a quieter moment plays with the London Philharmonic.

In Britain there were blues bands like Fleetwood Mac (Mark 1) and Chicken Shack, capitalizing on the audiences forged by John Mayall and Eric Clapton. There was the Mod rock of the Who and the Kinks, fantasy rock from Traffic, folk rock from Steeleye Span, Pentangle and Fairport Convention, fantasy folk rock from the Incredible String Band, comic rock from the Bonzo Dog Doo-Dah Band, bubblegum rock from the Bay City Rollers and Slik, glitter rock from Gary Glitter, and heavy metal rock from Led Zeppelin, Black Sabbath and Deep Purple.

In America, the early 60s' protest songs of Bob Dylan – 'Blowin' In The Wind', 'Masters Of War', 'The Times They Are A'Changin' ' – had become anthems of the growing peace movement. Their abrasiveness was sweetened by the Byrds, Joan Baez and, in their formative years, Simon and Garfunkel. Protest and nonconformity fed on them, finding a ready running target in the Vietnam war, in Chicago's brutal mayor Daley, in the shooting of students on college campuses. First Buffalo Springfield, and later Crosby, Stills, Nash and sometimes Young were the lyrical and respectable voices of young concern.

The hippie movement tried to find an alternative reality, delving, as the Beatles had, into Eastern mysticism, drugs and psychedelia. Flower power blossomed when Scott McKenzie invited everyone to come to San Francisco – and there acid rock groups like

270

Jefferson Airplane and the Grateful Dead blew young minds with electrifying combinations of music, lights and LSD. Anti-society cult-heroes sprang up and became martyrs when their lifestyles proved too extreme: Jim Morrison of the Doors, Janis Joplin of Big Brother and the Holding Company, the multi-talented and influential Jimi Hendrix.

Less demanding and controversial sounds were available too. Diana Ross and the Supremes and the Four Tops led a stream of chart-topping Tamla stars out of Detroit, MFSD and the Three Degrees put Philadelphia on the musical map, Nashville stars like Emmylou Harris, Dolly Parton and Tammy Wynette followed Johnny Cash's example of taking country up the pop Top Twenty, and the Beach Boys continued to lead the Los Angeles contingent. Soul turned to disco, ska and blue beat gave birth to commercial reggae, ballads competed with beat, protest vied with passion – and all found a profitable place in the best-seller lists.

The Beatles had transformed the finances of popular music, too. As both writers and performers they had become multi-millionaires, partly because their early hits and their potential for even greater things had enabled them to sweeten the initial 'penny a record' royalties contract with E.M.I. They had demanded, and received, a minimum royalty of ten per cent which earned them an astonishing $154 million in one five-year period alone. Thereafter, every artist wanted a percentage, and an increasingly hefty one. The record industry was awash with money because of unprecedented sales to an ever-growing audience, and companies paid up for fear of losing out. Breathtaking extravagance became the hallmark of the popular music business. Rock stars hardly out of their teens bought stately homes and castles, islands and helicopters. They travelled by limousine and private

Pink Floyd's progressive, psychedelic music resulted in totally new sound
effects which were combined with spectacular lighting and visual innovations.
Their albums, *Dark Side of the Moon* and *The Wall* (right) are brilliant musical
comments on the pressures of modern life and have stayed
in the charts for years.

jet. They made more money in a few hours than most men could hope to earn in a lifetime. They earned more than presidents or prime ministers.

Superstars and supergroups were created by fans and record companies, equally hungry – though for different reasons – for new excitement. Rod Stewart grew from guttural lead singer of the Faces to become a massively popular solo artist. David Bowie dazzled his army of admirers with a unique series of varying personas and theatrical effects. Elton John and his co-writer Bernie Taupin mixed gentle ballads with up-tempo rockers on staggeringly successful singles and albums. Jack Bruce, Ginger Baker and Eric Clapton teamed up to form Cream, building highly praised concert improvisations round such chart successes as 'I Feel Free' and 'Sunshine Of Your Love'. Jon Anderson's frail vocals and Rick Wakeman's keyboard artistry merged into Yes, Mick Jagger strutted through every change in fashion in front of the Rolling Stones.

And from the London 'underground' came Pink Floyd. Image-conscious EMI had created a new label, Harvest, for progressive music in order to combat a similar new label marketed by Philips. Pink Floyd, who had been signed earlier to Columbia and were London's premier psychedelic band, were then switched in order to launch the new label successfully. The group had developed spectacular lighting effects for their stage shows, and a complex sound system which enabled them to move noises around the auditorium. 'It sounds like hell,' wrote a *Sunday Times* critic who saw one of their 1972 concerts. 'The set is dominated by three silver towers of lights that hiccough eerie shades of red, green and blue across the stage. Smoke haze from blinding flares drifts everywhere. A harsh white light bleaches the faces of two of the four musicians to bone as they crouch among the cauldron drums and snaking circuitry of the sound equipment. Much of the music created by their two guitars, drums and assorted electronic keyboards is calculated and controlled. But it is overlaid with a maze of extra tapes which titillate the ears from all sides with extra-terrestrial electronic sounds, whispers, cries, snatches of prayers and the susurrant keening of wind and rain, all operated from a massive console in the stalls, like a mini-Houston space control centre.'

Pink Floyd soon produced an album which was not only a colossal seller, but was hailed as an artistic triumph. *Dark Side Of The Moon*, an hour-long cycle of songs on the melancholy themes of social deprivation, madness and the pressures of modern life, sold four million copies in the two years after its release, and stayed in the album charts for the whole of that period. It was to revisit those charts regularly for years to come. The themes continued through later Floyd albums such as *Wish You Were Here* and *The Wall*, and the band became consistently phenomenal money-earners throughout the world.

Floyd's early records took full advantage of the great technological advances available at EMI's Abbey Road studios. The Beatles had had to lock two four-track tape-machines together for *Sergeant Pepper*. But by the mid '70s, rock groups were using two 24-track machines locked together. They were able to build up recordings with layers of sound,

Queen, a group formed by four highly intelligent college graduates, combined musical virtuosity with a productive and highly sexual stage performance by lead singer Freddie Mercury. Their single, 'Bohemian Rhapsody', is thought by many to be the pop 'record of the decade'. ▶

The Rolling Stones, by now the grand old men of rock, finally joined EMI in the late seventies,
resulting in a resurgence of their energy and popularity.

rather like a painter in oils. Artists could play more than one instrument – in the case of *Tubular Bells* creator, Mike Oldfield, scores of instruments – or sing multi-track duets with themselves. And an extraordinary variety of exotic sounds were at their disposal, while most engineers at Abbey Road could still remember the days when bands who asked for a water effect were given a bowl of water.

Glam-rock gave record company balance-sheets a brighter look in 1974. EMI signed Queen, four highly intelligent and articulate college graduates who mixed high-camp satin stage costumes and overt sex-appeal with progressive musical ideas. Their albums *Queen II*, *Sheer Heart Attack* and *A Night At The Opera* made them the band of the moment, dominating both the singles and albums charts in a fashion that seemed to have died with the Beatles. Their single 'Bohemian Rhapsody', arguably the record of the decade, stayed at No. 1 for two months. Its first line could have summed up the feelings of many rock stars and record executives: 'Is this the real life, is this just fantasy . . .?'

Marc Bolan was another of EMI's glam-rock superstars. His band, Tyrannosaurus Rex, had been an underground cult success in the late '60s. With the new decade, he shortened its name to T Rex and made contact with the burgeoning teenybopper market. 'Hot Love' was the first of ten consecutive hits which made him one of the most glittering idols of the glitter idiom. When the release of one of his records was unavoidably delayed, tearful fans besieged record shops all over Britain.

Three of the Beatles virtually opted out of the '70s' music scene. John Lennon wrote and recorded 'Imagine' and 'Jealous Guy', dabbled in record production, notably with Harry Nilsson, in New York and California, then shut himself away for five years in New York's Dakota Buildings, devoting himself to wife Yoko and son Sean, and buying extra floors of the apartment block for such essentials as refrigerated fur-coat storage rooms. George Harrison produced two albums which proved that possibly he had been under-estimated musically as a Beatle, then issued others that suggested he had not been. He spent most of the decade as an introspective hermit in the English countryside, losing a wife to Eric Clapton and finding a South American beauty to share his increasingly private life. Ringo Starr released a few middle-of-the-road albums, then moved into films and tried to live up to the Beatle song he had sung, 'Act Naturally'. They not only put him in the movies, they introduced him to a second wife, beautiful screen-star Barbara Bach.

Only Paul McCartney continued as a full-time contributor to the pop industry. After two successful solo albums, he and wife Linda formed their own band, Wings, recruiting Denny Laine from another of the supergroups, the Moody Blues. McCartney went on to earn a mention in the *Guinness Book Of Records* as the most prolific hit-record writer in history. Lennon and many ex-Beatle fans may have cringed at 'Mull Of Kintyre' type songs . . . but McCartney's royalties from writing, recording and performing turned him into rock's richest musician. Shrewdly, he bought the rights to all Buddy Holly's songs when the copyright became available and quickly earned enough on them to repay his investment.

275

Of the four Beatles, only Paul McCartney with his newly formed group Wings, consistently remained an active, innovative and best-selling artist. Although the other three, especially John Lennon with his album *Imagine*, continued to record, real and sustained success eluded them as single performers.

When Wings toured America in 1976 – a tour that produced a live double-album – a chartered jet fitted with luxury beds flew the band and its entourage to either New York or Los Angeles after each performance, so Paul and Linda were not separated from their children for too long.

Many fans never gave up the faint hope that the Beatles might get together again. And record companies never gave up the impossible hope of finding another group like them. For a few glorious months in 1972, Capitol Records executives thought they had done it with a group called the Raspberries. The band, discovered playing in a nightclub in Kent, Ohio, deliberately set out to be like the Beatles in appearance, music and stage presence. And Capitol sank huge amounts of money into promoting them. A day in May was proclaimed 'Raspberry Day', and the famous Capitol Tower in Los Angeles – resembling a pile of records – was festooned with banners, balloons and buttons publicizing the event. Visitors and staff were served with raspberry ice-cream during the afternoon, and pressmen got the same treatment at a lavish reception thrown to introduce them to lead singer Eric Carmen and the rest of the boys.

The group's first album was issued with a sticker attached to the sleeve, pungently scented with raspberries. As a gimmick it was a great idea – customers could sniff out the record in their local store, and more than one disc jockey blurted over the air: 'Gee, this thing smells of raspberries!' When 'Go All The Way', the Raspberries' first single, made the charts, Carmen unashamedly described it as their 'I Want To Hold Your Hand'. But in the end the promotional gimmicks rebounded on Capitol. The music on the perfumed album was not a success, and inevitably the disc became known as the 'stinking record'. The very word 'raspberry' was synonymous in some countries with a vulgar expression of rejection. Just as Bruce Springsteen found the burden of being labelled the new Dylan too great before establishing himself in his own right, so the Raspberries had to ditch their Beatles image before achieving the recognition their musical abilities warranted.

The huge sums of money rolling in made gimmicks, like the Raspberries promotion, luxuries record companies thought they could afford. Worldwide sales by the mid '70s were around £5,000 million a year, and the top artists could expect to earn at least £1 million annually from disc sales alone. Companies had the financial leeway to gamble on new talent and new ideas. Even record company staff were carried away by the years of plenty. In the words of the Pink Floyd song, they were riding the gravy train. Executives adopted the extravagances of the stars they dealt with. Private jets and luxury hotel rooms were part of the job. Companies rivalled one another in a mad helter-skelter of prestige and one-upmanship.

At the annual Cannes conference of the International Record and Music Publishing Market (MIDEM), chauffeurs sat in limousines illegally parked outside the Carlton Hotel for a whole week, never asked to drive anywhere – because conference delegates never left the hotel. The cars were merely another status symbol, a symptom of an industry bloated with too much money for its own good. Anyone with eyes to see knew that the spend-free days were numbered, that it was all too good to last. Pop music had created a bubble for itself that took no account of outside factors.

Seven years into the '70s, that bubble began to burst. The British record-buying public, less convinced that financial success was the ultimate measure of quality than their North American counterparts, began to tire of some of the overnight-millionaire superstars who were not prepared to share the repressive taxation of Britain with their fans, who lost their creative drive in the lap of their new-found Californian luxury, who rested on their tinsel laurels while turning out shoddy records. Suddenly, value for money became a criterion for fans. They remembered the days when albums carried eight tracks a side – now some groups were down to four, and a not-very-good four at that. Youngsters began to feel they were being conned. Stars would start off with a couple of albums, where a lot of effort had clearly been involved; then, tied to contracts they could not wriggle out of, they would fulfil them with the minimum of interest and attention to detail.

Record companies, too, found get-rich-quick performers a problem. Huge sums were paid out to deter them from transferring to other labels, but the stars seemed too busy cashing their cheques to find time to get to the studio for the recordings their contracts stipulated.

All of this added up to a growing suspicion among the most important section of the record-buying public – the teenagers and those in their early twenties – that their so-called idols really wanted to have nothing to do with them. That feeling of distance and alienation was not helped by the way live performances, like almost everything else, had got out of hand.

In the early '60s, it was still possible for bands to hire a van, book a few hotel rooms and carry instruments into a local theatre. This gave fans all over the country a chance to see their heroes perform the records they bought so faithfully. By the '70s, many groups needed convoys of juggernaut lorries or jumbo jets to transport the tons and tons of sophisticated equipment they required. In a few cases – Genesis, ELO, Bowie, Pink Floyd, Queen and Paul McCartney's Wings – the concerts that resulted justified the expense. There were many more that did not . . .

Even with the groups that were worth hearing, there was another problem. The cost and logistics of moving and using the equipment made only the biggest venues – giant halls or football stadiums – economically feasible. Instead of driving into their own town centres, rock fans now faced journeys of considerable distances to see their favourites on their increasingly rare excursions into the provinces.

Bands on the road also required an army of technicians, managers, agents and hangers-on. Rock groups took over entire floors of hotels – and sometimes wrecked them. Money, booze, drugs, groupies – all were available in limitless supplies to the new giants of the pop-music industry. Such outrageous lifestyles had been supported by the ever-increasing

Punk rock, the music of protest against society by the young and alienated, achieved its short-lived apex in the Sex Pistols, a group whose personal history ended in tragedy and death.

sales of ever-more-costly records . . . now there were signs of consumer resistance and distaste.

Suddenly, the big record companies had to face the harsh realities of life in a world of recession. Buyers were no longer prepared to take a chance on the esoteric offerings of bands and soloists grown self-indulgent. Albums produced expensively over many months were no longer selling in sufficient numbers to justify – or even cover – the outlay. And disillusioned teenagers were turning elsewhere to find an alternative to their fallen idols . . . and in Britain, where most post-Beatle pop trends had begun, kids were turning to punk rock.

Kate Bush

Punk – born in New York City but allowed to develop in Britain – was the angry sound of the streets, loud, raw-boned, inarticulate and violent. To the new breed of British and European youngsters, it was a welcome blast of realism in a world which seemed to offer only the dole queue when they left school. They could identify with the sentiments of the songs, the unpolished presentation of the performers. Protest songs in the '60s had opposed the present, but offered a dream in its place: love, peace, unity. The punk protest sneered at the present – and had nothing to offer instead. The no-hope anarchy and pessimism caught the mood of the self-styled Blank Generation, just as Presley, the Beatles and Bob Dylan had provided an appropriate youth soundtrack in their time. Punks were almost proud that some of the early records issued by small independent companies were badly pressed, that their new idols were abysmal musicians . . . at least they were REAL.

280

In the late '70s and early '80s two young and beautiful British female singers burst upon the international scene,

Sheena Easton.

The record giants knew they could not ignore the new movement. It had proved it was music that sold. But their attempts to come to terms with it were painful . . . and expensive. EMI raised eyebrows by lashing out £50,000 to sign up an unruly four-man band formed by Chelsea clothes-shop proprietor Malcolm McLaren. The Sex Pistols, who included tearaways who proudly dubbed themselves Johnny Rotten and Sid Vicious, were more famous for spitting on their audience than entertaining them. And they delighted in outraging the nation by appearing on an early-evening TV show and hurling obscenities at the speechless interviewer. Such a shock was more than EMI's fairly sedate corporate constitution could stand. The company told the Sex Pistols to go, and they went, still clutching their £50,000 cheque – straight to A & M Records, a supposedly hip record company. But A & M tolerated the band's carefully choreographed excesses for an even

Steve Harley.

Little River Band.

J. Geils Band

Kenny Rogers.

Taste of Honey.

Creedence Clearwater.

shorter time than EMI had. Again the band was dumped, again with a fat advance cheque in their hands. Finally a third company, even hipper Virgin Records, were more 'understanding' and rushed out a record to capitalize on the Pistols' newly-found notoriety. 'Anarchy In The UK' soared into the charts.

The group were to hog the headlines for two years, offending the silent majority by making their own use of a picture of the Queen on the cover of one album, using an eight-letter word of dazzling vulgarity on the next. For the shrewd McLaren, any publicity was good publicity, even when it stank. The Sex Pistols' publicity was terrible and their records sold in large numbers.

Eventually the Pistols feuded and broke up. Rotten reverted to his original name, Lydon, and formed a less obnoxious band; and Vicious became the high priest of punk decadence, a drug-crazed anti-hero who finally stabbed his girlfriend to death in a cheap New York hotel room, then killed himself before his trial for murder.

But after the initial shock of the New Wave, technically more skilful, increasingly articulate and longer-lasting bands emerged: the Stranglers, the Clash, Jam, the Boomtown Rats in Britain and Blondie and the Motels in America. These bands matured into commodities that record companies could handle safely.

The punk movement in fact gave popular music the shot in the arm it needed: a new urgency and realism. Some bands even insisted on fixing the prices at which their albums could be sold, usually below the normal rate. And on the back of the new music came new sounds from the British streets: Midlands two-tone groups like the Specials and the Beat, the zany Madness and the New Romantic offerings of Duran-Duran, Spandau Ballet, Visage and Ultravox.

EMI rode out the Sex Pistols storm and dipped its toes into less controversial sounds. Some internationally established stars continued to sell well, among them Cliff Richard, Pink Floyd, Queen and Wings. Then in the late '70s the company signed the Rolling Stones and played a part in reinvigorating the grand old men of rock who in the latter half of 1981 earned £60 million during a marathon US tour, generating sales of £20 million for their album *Tattoo You*. And two new talented female singers burst upon the music scene, the weird and wonderful Kate Bush and the Glaswegian Sheena Easton. In the US the industry also picked itself up again after the many lean years, with such stars as Kenny Rogers, the J. Geils Band, rock veteran Bob Seeger and newcomers Billy Squire and Kim Carnes.

However, by the end of the '70s, record companies were beginning to experience more intractable problems than punks and over-indulgence, problems which threatened the very existence of the music machine itself. Disillusionment may have pricked the bubble of the golden years, but piracy and home taping of cassettes had become major factors behind the slump in record company profits. Counterfeited tapes and discs of best-selling albums, virtually indistinguishable from the real thing, had been worming their way into the legitimate market for years, and in their desperation companies introduced coloured vinyl

Kim Carnes.

Martha Davis of Motels.

Dr Hook.

Bob Seeger a recording artist whose chart success remains in the US although he has a huge
following in Europe with album sales. His rock classic 'Hollywood Nights' typifies his all-round
talent as musician/composer.

records, even discs with performers' pictures stamped under the grooves, in an effort to halt sliding sales. But neither gimmick worked.

Sound quality of records was also becoming a problem. Discs churned out by mass-production methods were struggling to match the technological advances in both recording and playback systems.

Although the music machine has survived all its feared rivals, from radio to magnetic tape, in the '80s progress could make the gramophone as we know it as obsolete as Thomas Edison's phonograph cylinder. Digital recording, a new technology of converting sound waves into numbers, has arrived and brought with it significantly reduced distortion, hiss and surface noise. A number of new systems for carrying digital audio information will be competing for industry and consumer acceptance – systems which include small discs which are read by lasers, standard video cassettes and compact video cassettes. These are the products of the so-called 'new technology'. Records will be played again and again, for ever, without wear, tear or scratch. Video cassettes and video discs will provide music-lovers with visual as well as aural stimulation and the gramophone will never be the same again.

Edward Bellamy wrote in 1887: 'It appears to me that if we could have devised an arrangement for providing everybody with music in their homes, perfect in quality, unlimited in quantity, suited to every mood, beginning and ceasing at will, we should have considered the limit of human felicity attained, and ceased to strive for further improvements.'

The music machine has far surpassed Bellamy's expectations.

◄Gradually, with the new technologies taking hold, records were being video-taped as well as recorded. In the future, with the arrival of video discs and similar innovations becoming a distinct possibility, performances would have to match musical quality for a band to stay on top, a development reminiscent of the movies going from silent films to talkies.
Such visually powerful groups as Pink Floyd and Queen were to be further enhanced and less well-known groups such as the Tubes, whose thematic stage performance has made them a cult group, also were to benefit. EMI Music took over the centre stage at Shepperton Studios for a week to video-tape the Tubes' latest album.

CREDITS

The caricatures and signatures on pages 86/119/121/163/248
are reproduced by courtesy of Sir Joseph Lockwood.

The author wishes to thank Bob Hart of EMI Music for his unstinting support and advice in creating this book. Special thanks to Bob are related also to keeping the bar adjacent to his office open in times of great stress and calumny.

Ken East and Roger Stubbs of EMI also much deserve the author's thanks for their continued enthusiasm for a project which seemed to never end and in Roger's case keeping track of endless details. Mike Allen, with his vast knowledge of classical music, also was of great assistance in pinning down dates and events that had been forgotten long ago.

Furthermore thanks are due to the many people at EMI who gave of their time and knowledge and sat still for long interviews. These include Sir Joseph Lockwood, Peter Andre, David Bicknall, Bob Dockerill, Len Wood, Harry Shaberman, and many others who if not mentioned have the author's apology.

The author finally wishes to thank Douglas Maxwell for the cover idea, which came out of a long conversation and proved the perfect solution. His recommendation of Graham Ovenden as the artist is also much appreciated.